UNTO US A CHILD IS BORN

D1558993

Unto Us a Child Is Born

Isaiah, Advent, and Our Jewish Neighbors

Tyler D. Mayfield

WILLIAM B. EERDMANS PUBLISHING COMPANY
GRAND RAPIDS, MICHIGAN

Wm. B. Eerdmans Publishing Co.
4035 Park East Court SE, Grand Rapids, Michigan 49546
www.eerdmans.com

26 25 24 23 22 21 20   1 2 3 4 5 6 7

ISBN 978-0-8028-7398-9

Library of Congress Cataloging-in-Publication Data

Names: Mayfield, Tyler D., 1980– author.
Title: Unto us a child is born : Isaiah, Advent, and our Jewish neighbors
    / Tyler D. Mayfield.
Description: Grand Rapids, Michigan : Wm. B. Eerdmans Publishing
    Company, 2020. | Includes bibliographical references and index.
    | Summary: "Explores passages from the book of Isaiah through
    the two Christian lenses of the liturgical season of Advent and the
    ethical obligation of love toward the Jewish neighbor"—Provided by
    publisher.
Identifiers: LCCN 2019054480 | ISBN 9780802873989
Subjects: LCSH: Bible. Isaiah—Criticism, interpretation, etc.
    | Advent. | Christianity and other religions—Judaism. |
    Judaism—Relations—Christianity.
Classification: LCC BS1515.52 .M38 2020 | DDC 224/.106—dc23
LC record available at https://lccn.loc.gov/2019054480

For Jude

What the "experts," with their overarching concern for historical critical material, have been doing with Isaiah in their commentaries, often has little or nothing to do with what the rest of the world has been doing with him, and still does, in literature, art, music, worship and politics.

John F. A. Sawyer,
The Fifth Gospel: Isaiah in the History of Christianity

For those who do interpretation—especially Christian interpretation—the Shoah stands as a dread-filled summons to unlearn a great deal. For Christians this means the unlearning of "final readings," for "final readings" tend, I suggest, to give ground for "final solutions."

Walter Brueggemann,
"A Fissure Always Uncontained,"
in *Strange Fire: Reading the Bible after the Holocaust*

Contents

Contents

Contents

Contents

Foreword

We Christians are learning, albeit belatedly, how much supersession-ism is inscribed in our liturgical cadences and our interpretive habits. We are becoming aware that our habits of reading the two biblical testaments as "promise and fulfillment" are inherently supersessionist as the Hebrew Bible (Old Testament) functions then as an anticipa-tory text that culminates in the reality of Jesus. We know, moreover, that such renditions of the biblical text in supersessionist categories inescapably lead to anti-Semitism based on the unspoken premise that the theological claims of Judaism no longer pertain.

Tyler Mayfield has directly addressed these concerns. He provides a way of being self-aware and self-critical of our Christian cadences and habits, and he opens a way for biblical interpretation that is not preemptive and exclusionary. His way of teaching us new perspec-tives is by giving attention to specific biblical texts that recur in the Christian lectionary that are so familiar to us that we do not notice how they may have been preempted. He usefully focuses on texts from the book of Isaiah, as Isaiah is especially prominent in our Christian usage. And he attends to Isaiah texts that the church reads in Advent with the unexamined assumption that the promissory texts of Isaiah lead directly to Jesus.

Mayfield's way with eight Isaiah texts that are especially familiar to the church is rich, imaginative, and thick with multiple meanings. In each case he first considers what is likely the historical context of the text in its original usage. In this he relies on a well-established critical consensus. He then considers how the text is read (or mis-read) in the New Testament usages. Thus, for example, concerning the anticipation of "the virgin" in Isaiah 7:14 he reflects on the way in which the Gospel of Matthew appeals to the Greek translation of Isaiah and then exercises great liberty in its reading of the Greek translation. Finally, he considers how the text is read through our contemporary Christian lectionaries. He notices the ways in which the Isaiah readings are grouped with other lectionary texts that tilt the Isaiah texts in fresh and suggestive ways that are not necessarily in sync with the original Isaiah text. Indeed, the lectionary committees have taken great imaginative liberty in grouping texts as they have. This pattern of three contexts—historical, New Testament, and contemporary lectionary—exhibits the way in which texts are laden with and permissive of a variety of readings that do not require a particular theological rendering that is predictably reductionist.

Mayfield's threefold approach is not rigid. Thus, for example, in considering the "great light" seen by God's people in Isaiah 9, his discussion turns to the Jewish celebration of Hanukkah and the resilient hope of Judaism. In his consideration of Isaiah 61 with its extravagant hope, Mayfield turns toward James Cone and Black liberation theology. In Isaiah 2 and its "swords and plowshares," Mayfield takes the oracle to be utopian so that the text invites a reflection on utopian literature and its dystopian counterpoint that is regularly a critique of present social reality.

Before he arrives at these specific text studies, however, Mayfield offers an extended, accessible seminar on the matter of Christian supersessionism that is compellingly undertaken. This extended introduction and the specific textual studies that traverse a variety of contexts together mean that the book is a most formidable invitation for those who want to learn to read more responsibly. Alongside the impact of Christian liturgy and the lectionary, this book recognizes that our reading is an ethical matter of loving our neighbors who, perforce, read the text very differently. Embrace of this ethical mandate is not easy, however, given the force of familiar liturgical cadences and the exclusionary assumptions that sustain those cadences. That mandate is nonetheless urgent. It strikes me that Mayfield's invitation to read differently is not simply a matter of checking the boxes on these particular texts. To do that is to misunderstand Mayfield. It is rather mustering doxological imaginative freedom to offer an open-ended reading that allows for and takes seriously readings other than our own. When this book is taken seriously, we may find ourselves resituated so that we will celebrate Advent and Christmas differently. We will not cease our joyous acknowledgement of the birth of Jesus and the world-changing impact of his birth. But we will notice alongside us other people of genuine faith who do not share that celebration. What we celebrate is from our own lived experience. It is no less so for our neighbors. Surely it is true that loving our neighbors through our reading of Scripture is to love God, who eludes even our best habits and our most treasured cadences.

Walter Brueggemann
Columbia Theological Seminary
June 4, 2019

Acknowledgments

The idea for this book arose in 2013 when, during the spring semester, I taught an advanced Hebrew exegesis course on Isaiah and a course on biblical interpretation after the Holocaust. Moving weekly between those two classes sparked my interest in this book's topic. I thank the students in those two courses for allowing me to bring ideas from one course into the other. Thank you especially to Rev. Elana Keppel Levy, whose insightful and challenging comments on an early draft of this book clarified my thoughts and strengthened my presentation of them. Thank you also to the Pathways Sunday School class of Second Presbyterian Church, Louisville, Kentucky, for listening to my nascent thoughts on this subject during Advent 2014. Thank you to two of my seminary students—Cinda King and Daniel Van Beek—who edited the entire book with thoughtful care, saving me from so many errors. Thank you to Bruce Maples for editorial comments and attention to commas.

Thank you to the Louisville Presbyterian Theological Seminary's Board of Trustees for granting me two sabbaticals to work on this project: in the spring semester of 2015, I began conceptualizing and writing this book, and in the spring semester of 2019, I completed the manuscript. My seminary faculty colleagues, expressly Shannon Craigo-Snell, Susan R. Garrett, and Carol Cook, encouraged me to take on the role of biblical theologian and move beyond the historical arguments. I am grateful to be a part of an academic community that values writing for the church.

I am thankful to count two brilliant Isaiah scholars as friends: Marvin Sweeney, my dissertation advisor, and Trisha Tull, my predecessor in the A. B. Rhodes chair for Old Testament at Louisville

Presbyterian Theological Seminary. I hope they find their influences in this work. For a more comprehensive reading of the entire book of Isaiah, one can consult their insightful commentaries. During graduate work, I was fortunate to enroll in two courses on Isaiah at Yale Divinity School, one with Carolyn Sharp and one with Christl Maier. My need to have Isaiah as a theological companion surely began in those classrooms.

Finally, I dedicate this book to my middle child, Jude Carter Mayfield. May you strive to live out Isaiah's vision of swords becoming plowshares!

Introduction

Each year when we adorn our churches with Advent wreaths and Nativities, we evoke the joyous words of the prophet Isaiah: "Behold, a virgin shall conceive, and bear a son, and shall call his name Immanuel" (7:14).[1] In this proclamation, we recognize a summary of the holiday season, one worthy of inscription on a Christmas card. Glancing at the tiny babe in the crèche, we long to experience God's presence and to hear the familiar narratives surrounding Jesus's unique conception. Isaiah's statement affirms these longings. The prophet of old reassures us that God is with us in the form of a son, God's son. Isaiah knows our story, our reason to celebrate with kids' pageants and the hanging of greens. Isaiah helps us tell our story during our month-long celebration of Advent.

Each December we hear another excellent word from Isaiah: "For unto us a child is born, unto us a son is given: and the government shall be upon his shoulder: and his name shall be called Wonderful, Counsellor, The mighty God, The everlasting Father, The Prince of Peace" (9:6).[2] We read this piece of Holy Writ with the eighteenth-century tune of Handel's *Messiah* helping the words linger in our choir stalls and religious imaginations. Isaiah's beautiful titles help us envision how the "hopes and fears of all the years are met in thee tonight."[3] His poetry brings the promises of Advent to fruition.

1. King James Version used here. A different translation will be presented in Chapter 3.
2. King James Version used here. A different translation will be presented in Chapter 4.
3. "O Little Town of Bethlehem," (no. 121) in *Glory to God: The Presbyterian Hymnal* (Louisville: Westminster John Knox, 2013).

Introduction

Yet a hint of hesitation remains as we hear these familiar Isaiah passages, for we also affirm that these words were uttered first to ancient people in need of comfort. They lived centuries before that auspicious night in Bethlehem. Isaiah, the eighth-century prophet, knows not our swaddled Christmas infant. He has not witnessed the cramped manger or seen the star overhead. Christians did not exist, much less celebrate Advent, during Isaiah's prophetic ministry. His young woman does not know Mary. His wonderful son is not our Jesus. Isaiah has no awareness of the hundreds of years of Christian tradition that would later interpret his message.

Moreover, what about the "us" in the prophet's proclamation, "For unto *us* a child is born, unto *us* a son is given"? Unto whom? Who do we think "us" is? Handel and Advent observances have an answer to this question: Christians are "us." However, what child is this for the ancient prophet Isaiah? Living hundreds of years before Jesus, would Isaiah have been thinking of another child? These are magnificent titles indeed for a child—the mighty God, the everlasting Father. But are they reserved only for Christians?

This hunch about another child and another woman lingers as we race forward to our current reality and religiously diverse world, a world where we live and work alongside Jewish friends. In their synagogues they too read Isaiah's prophecies, but they do not find the same meaning in them. How might Jews today understand Isaiah's "child"? If we regard Isaiah as speaking only of Jesus, as telling only our Advent story, then what does our interpretation say about our friends and contemporaries?

It is vital to affirm that God's presence—Immanuel—takes a different, but valid, form for our faithful neighbors. Moreover, we want to affirm our Christian readings of Isaiah as well. So how might we read Isaiah's prophecies for today? How are we to cherish these encouraging words from Isaiah amid Advent candle lightings and lengthening nights while also valuing the vibrant faith of Judaism?

May I recommend a pair of bifocals?

In this book, I invite you to view Isaiah through two lenses. We use our near vision to see how our Christian liturgical season of Advent shapes our readings of Isaiah, and we use our far vision to see how our religiously diverse world, including our relationship to Jews

2

and Judaism, shapes our readings of Isaiah. I invite you to recognize that we need both near vision and far vision to see Isaiah clearly and responsibly.

A Bifocal Look at Isaiah

How do we view Isaiah through the lens of the liturgical season of Advent? How might we see Isaiah through a lens of a Christian love ethic toward our Jewish neighbors? These two questions anchor this book, the very questions that lead us to a bifocal look at Isaiah. Why bifocals? Because we need to attend to two matters together; we need our near vision to see what is close to us as well as our far vision to see what is farther off. As worshipping Christians, we pay attention to what is close to us—our worship practices and our liturgical celebrations during various seasons of the Christian year. We pray and sing; we celebrate holidays. These are in our near vision. However, we also need to pay attention to the ways that our practices and interpretations affect those not within our communities. This is our far vision. If we are not careful, we may suffer from shortsightedness. We may overfocus on the use of Isaiah within our tradition and miss the repercussions of our actions. We may render Jews invisible or irrelevant or as incomplete Christians. Using bifocal lenses, we can read Isaiah as faithful Christians within Christian worship contexts, while also reading responsibly in ways that encourage us to love our non-Christian neighbors.

To use Isaiah responsibly during Advent, we need to ruminate more deeply on the significance of this liturgical season. What exactly are we celebrating during the season of Advent? Are we merely waiting for the birth of Jesus at Christmas, effectively limiting Advent to an invitation to think ahead, to prepare for the next church season? Alternatively, are there significant theological concepts embedded in this season? By understanding the advent of Advent, or at least the theological underpinnings of this liturgical season, we can begin to prepare space for the season to provide spiritual connections to our lives, connections that relate to the birth of Christ and connections that do not. Also, we need to think about how Isaiah fits into Advent's purpose and ethos. When does Isaiah appear in the lectionary? How might we read Isaiah through the lens of the theological insights of Advent?

The book of Isaiah is not guidance and inspiration for us alone. Through our long-distance vision, we need to see Isaiah as a shared biblical text, one not held exclusively as our own. If you open the Jewish Bible—some Jews call it the Tanakh or Mikra—you will find Isaiah among the *Nevi'im* (prophets) between Kings and Jeremiah. If you visit a Shabbat service at your local synagogue, you might hear Isaiah read as a complement to the Torah reading. We share Isaiah with our contemporary Jewish neighbors. They too have relied on the beloved prophet in their liturgical celebrations and theological musings. We might also imagine our ancient neighbors, the original audiences of the book of Isaiah, who saw in these words inspiration and guidance to pass on to the next generation. Isaiah stirred them as well.

We share Isaiah with our neighbors. This point is not to be lost among our celebrations of Advent. Even as we busy ourselves for the arrival of the Christ child, we are reminded we are neither the first nor the only ones to hear *our* stories in Isaiah's stories. How can we affirm our Christian understandings of Isaiah while also learning different understandings from the past and from contemporary Judaism? How can we shape our understandings of Isaiah in new ways, so we do not pretend to monopolize the book?

To proclaim the Christian message of Advent using Isaiah requires us to share our sacred literature. Why? Because reading and interpreting our stories of Scripture involve taking responsibility for our actions. Reading and interpreting are matters of ethics. In Scripture, we find the call to love our neighbor. Our readings of the Old Testament draw us closer to our neighbors and require of us thoughtful engagement with others. In a world of other religious faiths and spiritualities, the way we handle our sacred literature impacts the ways we think about our religiously "other" neighbors. Can we leave space in our Christian readings of Isaiah to remember we share this prophetic book with Jews?

This book reads selections from the book of Isaiah through two lenses: the liturgical season of Advent and the ethical obligation toward the Jewish neighbor. The first lens is the prevalent way Isaiah is presented to many Christians today. Advent is when, in our worship and devotions, we hear most clearly this Old Testament prophetic book. The second lens helps us rethink our traditional understandings of Isaiah's message in light of our commitments to the vitality of Judaism. The first lens signals the search for the distinctly Christian understandings of Isaiah; the second lens signals that Christian understandings of Isaiah cannot participate in harm toward Judaism. The first lens grounds us in a living religious tradition with a vibrant history of interpreting this biblical book. The second lens compels us to critique and reject some aspects of this tradition, those that are hurtful, inaccurate, and derogatory toward our religious neighbors. Both lenses push us beyond historical-critical understandings of the text while still appreciating the history of the text's interpretation. Both lenses open up explicitly theological understandings of Isaiah. Both lenses are necessary for our faith context as we feel the tension between identity within a particular faith tradition and openness to the faith traditions of others.

Of course, we know that liturgy and ethics are not easily separated. In her excellent and provocative book on racism and sexism in Christian ethics, Traci West notes, "The rituals of Sunday worship enable Christians to publicly rehearse what it means to uphold the moral values they are supposed to bring to every aspect of their lives, from their attitudes about public policy to their intimate relations."[4] We are searching for ways to bring these ways of viewing together in our readings of Isaiah. We want to be faithful to our ethics during our worship. We want our worship to spur us to live out our ethical claims.

Why Isaiah?

Christian readings of Isaiah did not begin yesterday or with the creation of the season of Advent. The book has gripped the Christian imagination for centuries, providing a wellspring of images to

---

4. Traci C. West, *Disruptive Christian Ethics* (Louisville: Westminster John Knox, 2006), 112.

help relay the events of the Christian story.[5] The process began in the first-century CE world: the New Testament quotes or alludes to the book of Isaiah more than any other part of the Old Testament (with the possible exception of the Psalms).[6] The Gospels, the Epistle to the Romans, and the book of Revelation also show a particular interest in the book. These New Testament books, written across multiple decades, by numerous authors, and in various locales, shared a striking concern for Isaiah.[7] Moving beyond the New Testament to later Christian literature, art, music, and liturgy, we learn that no other book in the Hebrew Scriptures, except the Psalter, has generated as much commentary and theological interpretation in the Christian tradition as Isaiah.[8] Today, Isaiah continues to influence the way Christians paint, sing, write, and worship. The message of Isaiah helps believers find a pew within the church's more substantial edifice of Scripture and seems a natural fit for the Christian story.

This natural fit partially explains the book's nickname: the Fifth Gospel. The moniker places Isaiah alongside the revered Matthew, Mark, Luke, and John, and it also highlights Isaiah's honored seat at the Christian theological table. Saint Jerome, the fourth- and fifth-century CE theologian and priest, affirmed Isaiah's exalted status and summarized well the prophet's role in what became the Christian tra-

---

5. See the brilliant analysis by John F. A. Sawyer in *The Fifth Gospel: Isaiah in the History of Christianity* (Cambridge: Cambridge University Press, 1996). See also Richard Beaton, *Isaiah's Christ in Matthew's Gospel*, Society for New Testament Studies Monograph Series 123 (Cambridge: Cambridge University Press, 2002).

6. Sawyer, *Fifth Gospel*, 21.

7. It is understandable that these authors would express interest in passages from the Hebrew Bible since they themselves were all Jews. My point here is that they were not equally interested in all sections of their canon. The New Testament authors draw from Deuteronomy, Psalms, and Isaiah much more than Esther, Song of Songs, and Ezekiel.

8. As one example, note the thirty-one homilies of Aelred of Rievaulx, a twelfth-century abbot, on Isaiah 13–16, which contains mostly oracles against nations. See Aelred of Rievaulx, *Homilies on the Prophetic Burdens of Isaiah*, trans. Lewis White, Cistercian Fathers Series 83 (Collegeville, MN: Liturgical Press, 2018).

dition, saying that Isaiah "should be called an evangelist rather than a prophet."[9] Isaiah, through an enduring process of interpretation surrounding the prophet's book, has become an evangelist for the good news of Jesus in a way unique among Old Testament prophets. The Christian tradition took Isaiah from his seat at the table of prophets, where he dined with Jeremiah and Amos, and placed him alongside Matthew and Mark. In this Christian understanding, Isaiah is not merely the most celebrated or beloved of the prophets; he heralds the good news of Christ.

We could explore many more stories about Isaiah's intersections with Christianity through the years, but our concerns lie elsewhere. This book focuses on contemporary interpretations of Isaiah as we celebrate Advent as Christians; it focuses on how we read faithfully and ethically in our time and place. In truth, at times our readings have been harmful. An excellent example comes from the earliest long-form instance of anti-Jewish polemic, Justin Martyr's *Dialogue with Trypho the Jew*. In this second-century CE Christian work, Saint Justin, a theologian, engaged in an imaginary dialogue with Trypho, a Jew. Justin argued Jesus was the Messiah and Christians were the people of God. It is apparent from the beginning Justin intended to convert Trypho, so "dialogue" might not be the best title for his work, but in the course of laying out his case for Christ, Justin quoted Isaiah more frequently and at greater length than any other book in the whole Christian Bible.[10] He showcased Isaiah more than the Gospels![11] The irony is thick: a Christian using a Jewish prophetic book to proselytize a Jew.[12] Irony aside, it is astounding how quickly the prophetic book of Isaiah became Christian evidence.

We do not see this type of harsh polemic in modern-day celebrations of Advent, nor do most Christians engage in such ex-

9. Cited in Steven A. McKinion, ed., *Isaiah 1–39*, Ancient Christian Commentary on Scripture: Old Testament 10 (Downers Grove, IL: InterVarsity, 2004), 3.

10. Sawyer, *Fifth Gospel*, 102.

11. Perhaps he did so because he believed that the Jews of his day would be more likely to accept one of their own sacred books than Christian literature.

12. The irony is all the sweeter when we take into account that Jesus was also Jewish!

plicitly anti-Jewish polemics or the desire for the conversion of Jews. Additionally, we do not use the sacred Scripture of Isaiah against the Jews to refute their claims or to highlight heresies. Fortunately, Jewish-Christian relations are not stuck in the second century CE. In light of the Holocaust, Christians have taken steps to rid ourselves of anti-Jewish statements in our official documents and unofficial educational materials.[13] We do not engage in polemic. However, our liturgy and preaching occasionally still fall into the traps of unintentional anti-Judaism. Our actual, on-the-ground practices have not caught up to our official statements and good intentions.

We could explore several practical examples here, but again, the focus of this book is Isaiah. A version of anti-Judaism, using Isaiah as if this prophetic book belongs solely to Christians, requires a subtle erasure of our sister religion. It entails an ignorance or silencing of Judaism's claim to Isaiah as Scripture. During Advent, it is tempting to regard Isaiah as Christian, as one of us. However, as we envision Isaiah's role, past and present, in Christianity, shifting our lens from Isaiah-as-prophet to Isaiah-as-evangelist no longer seems the appropriate posture for our religiously pluralistic world. Isaiah-the-evangelist transforms the prophet we share with Judaism into a Christian whom Jews do not share. Isaiah cannot be read as another Gospel such as Matthew, Mark, or Luke. By using Isaiah's rhetoric without care for Judaism's proper appreciation of their Jewish Bible, we may participate in harm toward our sisters and brothers.

In fact, and hopefully in practice, when Isaiah is appreciated as shared Scripture, it can function as an excellent model for learning between Jews and Christians. Isaiah has always had a prominent position within the Christian tradition; we should continue that legacy in preaching, worship, and study.

13. John Pawlikowski, "Accomplishments and Challenges in the Contemporary Jewish-Christian Encounter," in *Removing Anti-Judaism from the Pulpit,* ed. Howard Clark Kee and Irvin J. Borowsky (Philadelphia: American Interfaith Institute, 1996), 29–35.

A Story from the Rabbis

As Christians, we can learn great lessons from Jewish interpretation and its ability to bring forth new interpretations. A rabbinic parable exists about the need to read our Scriptures in transforming ways:

> By what parable may the question [of the difference between scripture and oral tradition] be answered? By the one of a mortal king who had two servants whom he loved. He gave a measure of wheat and a measure of flax to each. What did the clever one do? He took the flax and wove it into a tablecloth. He took the wheat and made it into flour, then kneaded the dough and baked it. He set the loaf on a table, spread the tablecloth, and waited for the king to come.
>
> But the foolish one did not do anything at all.
>
> After a while, the king came into his house and said to the two servants, "My sons, bring me what I have given you." One brought out the table with the loaf baked and the tablecloth. And the other brought out his wheat in a basket with the bundle of flax over the grain.
>
> What a shame! What a disgrace! Need it be asked which of the two servants was the more beloved? He, of course, who laid out the table with the loaf baked of flour upon it.[14]

The parable suggests that interpretation transforms the meaning of the biblical text in meaningful and beautiful ways. The transformation from wheat to bread is to be celebrated. Sometimes it may seem folks who dependably preserve the text entrusted to them are the most faithful. However, that "simpler" path requires little—no work, no creativity. We have been given the rich ingredients of wheat and flax—building blocks for life! The rabbis know God desires active participation to refine the product. This is our present task in an ever-changing world. We are makers of bread! We participate responsibly in the ongoing and never-ending interpretation of shared texts, and we read anew.

14. Paraphrased from Seder Eliahu Zuta 2, as recounted in Karin Zetterholm, "Jewish Interpretation of the Bible: Ancient and Contemporary," http://bibleinterp.com/articles/2013/zet378014.shtml.

Introduction

How to Read This Book

Part One of this book introduces a bifocal way of reading the book of Isaiah as a Christian: reading liturgically within the context of the practical, Christian celebration of Advent and reading ethically within the context of love for our Jewish neighbors. Chapter 1 attends to our near vision as we focus on the Christian liturgical season of Advent. As a step toward creating a Christian liturgical hermeneutics, we focus on four topics: (1) broadening Advent's theological framework beyond the two current theological emphases; (2) Advent's call for a reexamination of the relationship between the Old Testament/ Hebrew Scriptures and the New Testament/Christian Scriptures; (3) the Revised Common Lectionary's use of Isaiah during Advent; and (4) the problematic, traditional Christian notion of prophecy. Chapter 2 attends to our far vision as we focus on Christian love of our neighbors. As a step toward creating a Christian ethical hermeneutic of love, we focus on three elements of Christian readings of Isaiah: (1) the historical matter of messianism, (2) the theological problem of supersessionism, and (3) the ethical stance of anti-Judaism. Both lenses present challenges to old readings as well as opportunities for fresh understandings. They challenge us with new considerations while inspiring us with old deliberations.

Part Two engages a first set of Isaiah passages. Chapters 3 through 6 deal specifically with texts that are traditionally read as messianic: Isaiah 7:10–16; Isaiah 9:2–7; Isaiah 11:1–10; and Isaiah 61:1–4, 8–11. All share a concern with a single figure, a figure who at some point in our Christian history has been identified with the Messiah, the Christ, Jesus. These chapters examine the originating historical context for each passage as well as subsequent historical contexts, including how the passages took on messianic understandings. Additionally, I situate these passages within our contemporary context of today's world, particularly our celebration of Advent, thus demonstrating how the challenges and commitments of chapters 1 and 2 are brought to bear on biblical passages.

Part Three, which consists of chapters 7 through 10, deals with another set of Isaiah passages that are read as visions of the future: Isaiah 2:1–5; Isaiah 35:1–10; Isaiah 40:1–11; and Isaiah 64:1–9. These passages correspond to the other theological theme of Advent: the last things or eschatology. Again, I offer ways to read these texts within the frame of the Advent season and opportunities of neighborly love toward Jews. How might you use the three sections of this book? You could, of course, read straight through the book, taking in the theological frameworks of the first chapters and the interpretations of the remaining chapters. Individuals or groups who might enjoy that experience include readers who primarily are interested in Isaiah and/or Christian-Jewish relations and/or the season of Advent; readers who need maximum explanation about the topics of Isaiah, Advent, and Judaism; readers who prefer linear presentations; or people who need convincing evidence regarding the ethical implications of reading Isaiah in our religiously diverse world. However, many will want to treat this book as a resource, using selected chapters for preaching and teaching from Isaiah throughout many years. One of my aims in writing this book is that preachers and other religious leaders might feel empowered to discuss the text of Isaiah with religious communities. Fortunately, whether you read this work as a whole or in sections, Advent will come every year and the quest to understand the role of the book of Isaiah in our Advent seasons will endure.

Finally, all translations of Old Testament texts are mine unless otherwise noted. They are based on the Hebrew Masoretic Text as found in the Leningrad Codex, which dates to 1008 CE. My translations tend to follow Hebrew word order and phrasing, occasionally at the cost of standard English syntax. If you are looking for an acceptable English translation to read aloud in public settings, then I recommend the New Revised Standard Version or the Common English Bible. I have chosen throughout this book to translate the personal name for God, YHWH, as "The Living God" instead of the LORD, as is common in most English translations. Many complex issues arise when discussing the names of God. I have chosen this unique translation of YHWH for two main reasons: (1) "the LORD" has become so familiar a name as to be almost devoid of meaning, and (2) "the LORD" is both hierarchical and masculine.

PART ONE

Isaiah through Bifocals

ONE

Using Our Near Vision during Advent

My thoughts and feelings seem to be getting more and more like those of the Old Testament, and in recent months I have been reading the Old Testament much more than the New. It is only when one knows the unutterability of the name of God that one can utter the name of Jesus Christ; it is only when one loves life and the earth so much that without them everything seems to be over that one may believe in the resurrection and a new world; it is only when one submits to God's law that one may speak of grace; and it is only when God's wrath and vengeance are hanging as grim realities over the heads of one's enemies that something of what it means to love and forgive them can touch our hearts. In my opinion it is not Christian to want to take our thoughts and feelings too quickly and too directly from the New Testament.

Dietrich Bonhoeffer, a letter from prison,
Second Sunday of Advent, December 5, 1943

We need Isaiah to celebrate Advent. The book's treasures are too marvelous to set aside as ancient history or consign to another liturgical season. As we begin the liturgical year, we need to hear of swords beaten into plowshares and of barren lands blooming. During the season of Advent, it might be easier to steer a course straight through the Gospel readings, without veering to the Old Testament readings, but I cannot recommend such an itinerary.[1] To use only the Gospel readings during Advent limits our theological reflections while also insinuating that only those four biblical books are worthy of public reading and proclamation. Advisedly, we read the full canon of Scripture during our liturgical seasons.[2] Advent needs the stories of Israel as well as the stories of Jesus.[3] Advent, as a designed time during the church year, connects us to both sets of stories so we also might engage our own Advent stories.

In this chapter, I conjoin the biblical book of Isaiah and the liturgical season of Advent by discussing four issues that arise when we read Isaiah during Advent: (1) the mixture of dissonant theological emphases during our current celebration of Advent and how we might broaden Advent's theological register; (2) the relationship between the two testaments in the Christian Bible; (3) the Revised Common Lectionary's use of Isaiah; and (4) the problematic notion of prophecy as future-telling. As we connect our rich biblical tradition to contemporary worshipping communities, we need a more definite sense of the shape and effect of these four issues on our read-

1. Gordon W. Lathrop, *Saving Images: The Presence of the Bible in Christian Liturgy* (Minneapolis: Fortress, 2017), 129, notes, "It remains true that all three readings in the RCL [Old Testament, Gospel, and Epistle] should be used—or, in serious necessity, at least two. The very interactions and mutual dialogue of the readings, their juxtaposed images, and the space between them function as a deep part of the lectionary design. To choose only one of the readings is to abandon that design, acting rather in favor of the idea of scripture having a single voice, a single narrative of salvation, when the fascinating truth is that there are many voices."

2. It is unfortunate that the Revised Common Lectionary replaces the Old Testament lesson with a lesson from Acts during Easter. I am afraid the unintended (and erroneous) consequence is to communicate that the theological themes of resurrection and new life are not available to us in the Old Testament.

3. George Lindbeck, *The Nature of Doctrine: Religion and Theology in a Post-liberal Age* (Louisville: Westminster John Knox, 1984), 34, noted, "To become a Christian involves learning the story of Israel and of Jesus well enough to interpret and experience oneself and one's world in its terms." While this quote speaks to theological method foremost, I am always delighted to remember that Lindbeck includes not only the story of Jesus but the story of Israel as an object of learning.

ings. Unexamined and readily assumed during Advent, our inherited faith, rituals of celebrations, assigned biblical passages, and cultural understandings have combined in ways that perpetuate this lack of engagement with these issues. As religious leaders and caring Christians, we are not to blame for this deficiency, but we are responsible for engaging them as we move into an increasingly religiously diverse world, an engagement which might lead us to new places and fresh understandings of both the season and the Bible.

A Peculiar Convergence of Two Theological Emphases

Advent proclaims two theological themes: the coming of Christ as a child and the future coming of Christ at the end of time. A first coming and a second coming. Incarnation and eschatology. These two foci do not naturally cohere. The emotions invoked by Advent call us to "prepare joyfully for the first coming of the incarnate Lord and to prepare penitently for the second coming and God's impending judgment."[4] Joy and penitence. Alternatively, as our hymns resound, "Joy to the World! The Lord is Come" and "Lo, He Comes with Clouds Descending." It is a tense relationship to maintain within a single four-week period, a "season under stress."[5] We are pulled in different emotional directions. No wonder we are so confused about Advent celebrations!

Moreover, no wonder the pressure of Christmas—both as the next liturgical season in the Christian year and as American culture's obsession during December—leads us to emphasize more the joyful elements of Advent than the penitent. In our self-help society, it seems more natural to focus on the jubilant aspects of Advent and leave behind the tension of joy and penitence. We have, of course, a genuinely penitent season in our observance of Lent, so why not save the remorse for then? No matter how much we intuitively or intentionally emphasize one theme over another, our hymns and

4. Gail R. O'Day, "Back to the Future: The Eschatological Vision of Advent," *Interpretation* 62, no. 4 (October 2008): 357.
5. The phrase is taken from Richard C. Hoefler, *A Sign in the Straw* (Lima, OH: CSS, 1980), vii.

Scripture readings, our choral pieces and liturgies, are attuned to the tension present within the season. J. Neil Alexander expresses the tension thus:

> Is Advent a preparatory fast in preparation for the liturgical commemoration of the historical birth of Jesus in Bethlehem, or is Advent a season unto itself, a sacrament of the end of time begun in the incarnation and still waiting on its final consummation at the close of the present age? Is the content of Advent's proclamation centered in eschatological dread, judgment, and condemnation or eschatological hope, expectation, and promise? Is Advent really the beginning of the annual cycle or does Advent bring the year to a conclusion? The fact is that each of these "either/ors" are really "both/ands."[6]

Historically, how did these two different themes end up in this one liturgical season? Advent was one of the last major liturgical seasons to develop in the church year (following Easter, Christmas, and Lent). Liturgical scholars note that, before the introduction of the season of Advent, the time at the end of the liturgical (and secular) year was generally concerned with last things.[7] To focus on such eschatological matters was appropriate for this end-of-year, unofficial liturgical season within the church. As the liturgical year drew to a close, the church turned its attention to end-of-time matters before beginning the year again with Christmas. This eschatological vision with its accompanying discussion of the second coming of Christ provided a penitential element to this time of the year.

The Scripture readings and theological themes remain in our current lectionary to this day. Why? Why did penitence and eschatology continue to grasp the theological imagination of Advent as it developed into a liturgical season? One suggestion is that the theme of pen-

6. J. Neil Alexander, "A Sacred Time in Tension," *Liturgy* 13, no. 3 (1996): 5–10.

7. Horace T. Allen Jr., "Calendar and Lectionary in Reformed Perspective and History," in *Christian Worship in Reformed Churches Past and Present*, ed. Lukas Vischer (Grand Rapids: Eerdmans, 2003), 401–2.

itence was incorporated into Advent as a way for the church to prepare for Christmas. Just as the church prepared for Easter with a season of Lent, the church began to prepare for Christmas with a multi-week time of reflection. Yet, this season could not sustain a wholly penitent nature because of the need to begin the turn toward the theological themes of Christmas. Penitence—a theme of the end of the liturgical year—then combined with the theme of Christmas joy.

Advent, including its lectionary readings, incorporated both an emphasis on Jesus's nativity and a penitential, eschatological theme. It is difficult to precisely discern which theme came first, but I suspect the newer theme is the theme of joy, of preparing for Christmas's celebration of the incarnation within a liturgical cycle previously focused exclusively on the end things. The result is our current dual focus. As Horace Allen notes, "How strange, in a Reformed congregation, on the first Sunday of Advent, to begin with the lighting of an Advent wreath candle to mark the number of days until the Nativity, and then to hear as the Gospel lesson, 'watch and pray, for *no one knows* the day or the hour'!"[8] Strange indeed, but it is our contemporary liturgical situation. According to historical sources on the liturgical year, the church has never been able to settle on a single theme for this season. We count down the days to Christmas joy and await eschaton's judgment. J. Neil Alexander captures the tension and positive response:

> We could have settled for a severe, Lent-like period of disciplined preparation overcast by eschatological dread. By contrast, we could have settled for a joyful period of anticipation and longing founded upon eschatological promise. But these are not mutually exclusive ideas. Each represents only part of the revelation of God in Christ. To whatever degree we attempt in our liturgies or by our preaching to alleviate Advent's tension is the degree to which we rob ourselves

8. Allen, "Calendar and Lectionary," 402. J. Neil Alexander, in *Celebrating Liturgical Time: Days, Weeks, and Seasons* (New York: Church Publishing, 2014), 44–45, notes that the Advent wreath is "a mid-twentieth century adaptation for liturgical use of a domestic devotion that has roots in the pietistic traditions of seventeenth-century Germany."

of the incredible richness and grace that result from the annual eschatological collision in the weeks before Christmas.[9]

Despite this tension between the first coming and the second coming, we have found ways in our churches today to mix and match these elements under the umbrella term "waiting." We bid ourselves to wait. Advent is anticipation. Waiting for the baby Jesus and waiting for Christ, the judge. This emphasis provides a degree of cohesion to the lectionary readings. Some readers undoubtedly may have found the earlier discussion of joy and penitence rather odd as they have typically associated Advent with the theme of "waiting." Waiting makes sense of the dual aspects of the season. We light the Advent wreath candle each week to help us mark time as we wait. My local congregation used the theme "Pregnant with Possibility" for Advent recently, a phrase that surely connotes waiting excitedly for the arrival of something new.

Theologian Amy Plantinga Pauw helpfully brings forward the theme of longing for consideration during the season of Advent by noting, "Longing for God is a permanent feature of church life on earth."[10] Thus, she turns our waiting into a desirous activity, a posture of urges and eagerness. She suggests this longing occurs because the church recognizes Christ has come indeed, yet the world's ills also demonstrate the need for Christ's presence.

Alternatively, we might speak of hope as a unifying element bringing our different Advent themes together. We have hope in what the incarnation brings to our world each day, even as we hope for the setting right of things with the culmination of history. This theme takes seriously Advent's orientation to future events and its unwillingness to focus only on current reality. To hope is to dream of a new way, a way revealed in and through Jesus.

The advantage of themes such as *waiting, longing,* and *hope* is that they are general enough to encompass the tension we experi-

---

9. J. Neil Alexander, *Waiting for the Coming: The Liturgical Meaning of Advent, Christmas, Epiphany* (Washington: Pastoral, 1993), 24.

10. Amy Plantinga Pauw, *Church in Ordinary Time: A Wisdom Ecclesiology* (Grand Rapids: Eerdmans, 2017), 120.

ence during this season. To lead congregants through this theological tension requires agility and clarity about the liturgical arc of the season and how the teacher or preacher might effectively incorporate elements of joy and penitence. It is not enough to sound the isolated theme of penitence during the First Sunday of Advent, when it is most apparent, only to drop the theme for the following three weeks as the frenzied march toward Christmas quickens. It is also not helpful to allow the two themes to appear in worship and liturgy without some prior preparation. One can only imagine a service in which the joyful sounds of a given hymn are juxtaposed awkwardly with a reading about the end of the world!

We must also be aware of the other theological concerns of Advent. Advent is not solely about waiting. Advent is not just about fulfillment and hope. It does not have to be merely a wait-and-see month of Sundays for the church as we anticipate Christmas. We would not want to proclaim during Advent—when church attendance can be slightly higher than usual—that we are merely waiting. The gospel, the commonwealth of God, is here among us already—now!

In this book, and particularly in the readings from Isaiah in the following chapters, I want to move us toward appropriate liturgical shaping in which a wide range of Advent's theological themes are appreciated. This liturgical hermeneutic will explore beyond the typical christological approaches to the season to address additional theological issues. The texts from Isaiah are not all concerned with a messiah. Some are beautiful visions of the future, visions which include longing and joy. I will highlight Isaiah's understandings of hope and waiting, draw out his longing as a model for our longing, and invite Isaiah to bring depth to our waiting as we ponder both joy and penitence in this prophetic literature.

Old and New Testaments: The Problematic Prophecy-Fulfillment Paradigm

In addition to wrestling with the confluence of theological themes, we will receive an opportunity to reflect on the relationship between the two testaments during this liturgical season. Advent, more than any other season of the Christian year, demands a clear and theologically robust understanding of the relationship between the Hebrew Scriptures (Old Testament) and the Christian Scriptures (New Testament).[11] Ideally, every liturgical season is an opportunity to use the resources of the entire biblical canon. For example, Lenten themes are undoubtedly present in both Joel and Luke. However, Advent has the unique challenge of imagining Christ's absence both theologically and liturgically. We sing "O Come, O Come, Emmanuel" as an expression of this yearning in the face of absence. To better understand this time of anticipation, we turn naturally to the stories of the Hebrew Scriptures. In the overall biblical story, the Old Testament provides a backdrop for this time of longing.

Whenever we read and interpret Old Testament and New Testament passages together in a liturgical setting, we must be aware of how we present the relationship between these two sections of our Christian Bible. Our practices shape our theology. Our handling of the testaments, especially when presented as related to one another, embeds a theology of Scripture in us.[12] Although we may not intend to communicate explicitly the relationship between the testaments, assuming instead that our message of good news is more about God and Advent, we are sending a message of Scripture's rich canon whenever we bring its various sections into conversation with each other. We have some issues to consider when exploring the relationship between the Old Testament and the New Testament. We could, for example, examine how recent neo-orthodox christological approaches by theologians such as Karl Barth and Brevard Childs argue that both testaments share in their witness to Jesus. In other words, we could problematize this understanding of the testaments as united in their shared subject matter of Christology.[13] However,

---

11. The terminology for these two testaments is debated. I find no easy solution, so I will use a variety of names for the Hebrew portions of Scripture including Old Testament, Hebrew Bible, Hebrew Scriptures, and Tanakh.

12. An unrelated example: Some congregations stand for the reading of the Gospel lesson but not for the reading of the other lessons (Old Testament, Psalm, and Epistle). What does this earnest action communicate about certain sections of Scripture?

13. Brent A. Strawn, "And These Three Are One: A Trinitarian Critique

given our emphasis on Advent, I will focus here on the example of how the relationship between the two testaments is often framed problematically concerning the issue of prophecy and fulfillment.

Advent, as a season of waiting, often portrays Old Testament passages as the site of that waiting process, while New Testament passages are depicted as the culmination of the waiting. We assume that the Old Testament waits for what the New Testament brings. We might call this interpretive paradigm "prophecy-fulfillment."[14] The season of Advent can perpetuate this prophecy-fulfillment paradigm by reading the Old Testament lessons as unfulfilled prophecy, waiting on the arrival of Christ to reach their true fulfillment. In this paradigm, the Old Testament is heard not as a helpful word for today but as an incomplete word from yesterday.

What is so theologically problematic about the prophecy-fulfillment paradigm? First, it assumes a narrow perspective on Old Testament prophecy, namely, that prophecy is a prediction of the long-term future. However, Isaiah (or any other ancient Israelite prophet) provides little indication that he is predicting the far-off future. Instead, he is attempting to communicate a reliable message to his contemporary audience regarding their current situation. In other words, the prophetic literature of the Hebrew Scriptures is not concerned primarily with predicting a distant future. This genre of literature addresses the real theopolitical issues of the day; the prophets speak into their current situations, providing divine guidance and sanction to the people and political leadership. They are not concerned about events six centuries later. To read the Hebrew prophets as distant future-tellers is to stretch historical credibility. To read the Hebrew Scriptures within a prophecy-fulfillment paradigm is to misrepresent their self-understanding. I will return to this critical issue at greater length later in this chapter.

A second problem with the prophecy-fulfillment scheme is that the

---

of Christological Approaches to the Old Testament," *Perspectives in Religious Studies* 31, no. 2 (2004): 191–210.

14. There are other problematic models for the relationship between the Old and New Testaments (for example, a contrast model that heightens the theological differences between the two testaments in order to demonstrate the superiority of the New Testament). I have chosen to focus on the prophecy-fulfillment paradigm because of its association with Advent.

theological emphasis of such a paradigm falls on the fulfillment side of the equation. Theologically speaking, fulfillment or completion is better than a prediction. Unfulfilled prophecies are not nearly as theologically helpful as fulfilled prophecies. Hence, the New Testament comes to take precedence over the Old Testament. Alternatively, to provide some nuance, the fulfillment in the New Testament is taken more seriously than the prophecy in the Hebrew Scriptures. In fact, in the prophecy-fulfillment paradigm, the prophecy needs fulfillment in order to make complete sense. Without its fulfillment, prophecy remains incomplete. Sometimes an analogy is made to seed and flower in order to illustrate this point. The Old Testament is characterized as the seed, as in Philip Yancey's popular book *The Bible Jesus Read*: "In the writings from this [Old Testament] period lay the seed, but only the seed, of God's grace."[15] However, what good is a seed that does not flower? The seed needs to mature. It needs fulfillment or flowering.

Unfortunately, the paradigm often forces us to ignore how the Old Testament passage (prophecy) stands on its own without reference to a New Testament passage. The paradigm encourages us to allow the New Testament to set the parameters for interpreting the Old Testament, yet never encourages the opposite direction of dependence. (Would we ever claim that a New Testament passage plants a seed that ultimately flowers in the Old Testament?) We can allow a passage from the Hebrew Scriptures to stand alone, even prophecy. Every prophetic text does not need a partner text to provide explicit fulfillment.

The prophecy-fulfillment paradigm can also create a theological sense that the prophecy does not speak into our contemporary situation. This way of reading the prophetic text emphasizes its fulfillment. And what can we do with an already fulfilled text except admire it historically? How can it speak into our situations if its truest fulfillment has been found earlier in history? Ellen Davis notes, "We like to keep the frame of reference for prophecy within the 'safe' confines of the Bible, by reading prophecy solely as illuminating what has already happened—the birth, life, and death of Jesus Christ—and not

---

15. Philip Yancey, *The Bible Jesus Read* (Grand Rapids: Zondervan, 1999), 12–13. Cited in Strawn, "And These Three Are One," 197–98.

allowing it to meddle much in the current lives of Christians."[16] The language and theology of prophecy and fulfillment create a mostly closed system. One text directly points to another text and creates a closed loop making it difficult to apply to current situations.

The season of Advent provides opportunities for us to think about our relationship to the Old Testament. In this season of expectation, it is only fitting to draw upon the resources of the Hebrew Scriptures in order to set the stage for the birth of Jesus. The stories of Israel are relevant to the story of Jesus. We should not shy away from the Old Testament while telling the story of Jesus. The untold riches of the Old Testament are appropriately considered in conversation with the stories of the New Testament.

Shifting our focus from a more linear approach to the narrative of Scripture (in which we read the biblical books as a progression both in time and in theological depth) to a more back-and-forth conversational approach (in which we allow various texts to speak to one another) requires intentionality. It requires us to think about the relationship between the Old and New Testaments in a more complicated way—not as just a straightforward presentation in which the Old Testament provides "background" or even "foundational" material for the New Testament. A New Testament passage is not theologically superior to an Old Testament passage simply because of its placement in the New Testament section, or its authorship later in time, or even its mention of Jesus. Wisdom and revelation are found throughout both testaments.

This paradigm of understanding the testaments is consistent with Erich Zenger's proposed "hermeneutic of canonical dialogic discourse," which offers a way forward despite its complicated title.[17] He emphasizes how the two testaments function together as one Christian Bible and how the reader can bring into conversation texts from the two testaments without either taking precedence. They are

16. Ellen F. Davis, *Biblical Prophecy: Perspectives for Christian Theology, Discipleship, and Ministry* (Louisville: Westminster John Knox, 2014), xii.

17. Erich Zenger, *Einleitung in das Alte Testament* (Stuttgart: Kohlhammer, 2012), 21. Thanks to my colleague Johanna Bos for introducing me to Zenger's work and this particular concept. It is unfortunate that more of his work has not been translated from German into English for a larger audience.

equal partners with equal status as Scripture. Allen and Holbert describe the relationship between the testaments as follows: "The Hebrew Bible is the Holy Root from which grow the Holy Branches of the New Testament. We affirm that both testaments are holy, equally revelatory, equally expressive of the presence, purpose, and power of the God of Israel and Jesus of Nazareth."[18] Together the two testaments create a polyphonic text that speaks with many voices. These voices need to be placed into conversation with each other but not in a way that foresees the New Testament as the dominant voice.[19]

Advent and the Lectionary

The third issue related to Advent and Isaiah concerns the Revised Common Lectionary.[20] When we explore the lectionary Scripture lessons for Advent, we find a method (and a history) to its madness, but it is not always clear when looking at a single year's lessons. However, when we take a step back and look at the whole three-year cycle

18. Ronald J. Allen and John C. Holbert, *Holy Root, Holy Branches: Christian Preaching from the Old Testament* (Nashville: Abingdon, 1995), 16.

19. The Pontifical Biblical Commission, *The Jewish People and Their Sacred Scriptures in the Christian Bible* (Rome: Vatican Press, 2001), II, A, 5, §21, addresses this issue as follows: "The notion of fulfillment is an extremely complex one, one that could easily be distorted if there is a unilateral insistence either on continuity or discontinuity. Christian faith recognizes the fulfillment, in Christ, of the Scriptures and the hopes of Israel, but it does not understand this fulfillment as a literal one. Such a conception would be reductionist. In reality, in the mystery of Christ crucified and risen, fulfillment is brought about in a manner unforeseen. It includes transcendence. Jesus is not confined to playing an already fixed role—that of Messiah—but he confers, on the notions of Messiah and salvation, a fullness which could not have been imagined in advance; he fills them with a new reality; one can even speak in this connection of a 'new creation.' It would be wrong to consider the prophecies of the Old Testament as some kind of photographic anticipations of future events. All the texts, including those which later were read as messianic prophecies, already had an immediate import and meaning for their contemporaries before attaining a fuller meaning for future hearers. The messiahship of Jesus has a meaning that is new and original."

20. There are other lectionaries; yet I choose to focus on the Revised Common Lectionary because of its popularity.

of readings for this season, a certain pattern emerges. Every First Sunday of Advent (Years A, B, and C) includes an eschatological passage for the Gospel reading with complementary readings from the Old Testament and the Epistles.[21]

FIRST SUNDAY OF ADVENT

Year A	Matthew 24:36–44	Isaiah 2:1–5	Romans 13:11–14
Year B	Mark 13:24–37	Isaiah 64:1–9	1 Corinthians 1:3–9
Year C	Luke 21:25–36	Jeremiah 33:14–16	1 Thessalonians 3:9–13

All three passages from the Gospels—Matthew 24, Mark 13, and Luke 21—refer to the Son of Man's return. So be ready! We do not know the day or hour!

The Second and Third Sundays of Advent center on John the Baptist's ministry in the Gospel readings; they ring with an apocalyptic tone ("Prepare the way!") but also relate well to the coming of Jesus. On the Second Sunday, Jesus is spoken about indirectly as the one who is to come; he is not an actor in the story. On the Third Sunday, Luke and John tell another prebaptism of Jesus story, while Matthew includes an exchange between John the Baptist and Jesus.

SECOND SUNDAY OF ADVENT

Year A	Matthew 3:1–12	Isaiah 11:1–10	Romans 15:4–13
Year B	Mark 1:1–8	Isaiah 40:1–11	2 Peter 3:8–15a
Year C	Luke 3:1–6	Malachi 3:1–4	Philippians 1:3–11

---

21. I have left out the Psalm lesson in order to simplify this particular discussion. I would, of course, encourage Christians to read the Psalms during worship.

THIRD SUNDAY OF ADVENT

Year A	Matthew 11:2–11	Isaiah 35:1–10	James 5:7–10
Year B	John 1:6–8, 19–28	Isaiah 61:1–4, 8–11	1 Thessalonians 5:16–24
Year C	Luke 3:7–18	Zephaniah 3:14–20	Philippians 4:4–7

The Fourth (and final) Sunday of Advent sounds forth with anticipation for the arrival of the Christ child. Angels appear. Mary is with child. The birth is upon us. All the Gospel readings are taken from the first chapter of Matthew or Luke.

FOURTH SUNDAY OF ADVENT

Year A	Matthew 1:18–25	Isaiah 7:10–16	Romans 1:1–7
Year B	Luke 1:26–38	2 Samuel 7:1–11, 16	Romans 16:25–27
Year C	Luke 1:39–45	Micah 5:2–5a	Hebrews 10:5–10

We might conclude from this quick tour of the Advent lectionary Scripture lessons that the two Advent themes discussed above are intertwined but that penitence arrives first and fades eventually, while joy at the newborn child arrives later in the season. We also see that John the Baptist is featured prominently during this season as a way to conjoin penitence and joy.

How does the Revised Common Lectionary wish to bring together the book of Isaiah and the two themes of Advent? Simply put, the lectionary presents both themes with its selection of Isaiah readings for Advent. For example, the First Sunday of Advent in Year A prescribes Isaiah 2:1–5 as the Old Testament reading. It is a future-oriented prophetic oracle with eschatological possibilities. The passage envisions different groups streaming to the mountain of God in order to learn God's way with the result that swords are beaten into plowshares. Yet, by the Fourth Sunday of Advent in that same year, the congregation hears the Isaiah 7 prophecy of a pregnant woman and her child, Immanuel. Selections from the book of Isaiah are used, then, by the lectionary to develop both themes of joy and penitence. Isaiah 11 in the lectionary envisions the peaceable kingdom inaugurated by Christ. Isaiah 35 dreams of a future in which the desert shall blossom.

How exactly does the lectionary connect the book of Isaiah and the season of Advent while addressing these themes?

The Revised Common Lectionary, currently a staple in many mainline congregations, uses Isaiah extensively during Advent (and Christmas).[22] Seven out of the twelve possible Old Testament readings for Advent come from Isaiah. Given preachers' growing reliance on the lectionary, Isaiah receives a significant hearing in Advent worship services. During Year A, Isaiah is read every Sunday of Advent. Year B sees Isaiah read three out of four Sundays. Both years then provide an opportunity to feature Isaiah as "the prophet of Advent."

Critics of the lectionary raise valid questions concerning its effect upon the congregation as they repeatedly hear the same passages. Also, the Revised Common Lectionary omits certain biblical passages generally considered too violent or problematic both ethically and theologically. I am not unaware of these critical concerns. In many ways, I would be in favor of a revision or complete overhaul of the Revised Common Lectionary.[23] However, on a practical level, the lectionary has been around for over forty years now, and we see its influence only growing. Worship leaders now have many resources online and in print based on the Revised Common Lectionary. While we may want to nominate certain passages from the Old Testament for inclusion in a revised lectionary, for now, the reality is that the Revised Common Lectionary's popularity wanes not.[24] As a result,

22. I encourage preachers and other religious leaders who regularly use the Revised Common Lectionary to read the Introduction to the Revised Common Lectionary on the commontexts.org website: http://www.commontexts.org /rcl/RCL_Introduction_Web.pdf.

23. For an example of the issues the lectionary presents to Jewish-Christian relations, see Michael Peppard, "Do We Share a Book? The Sunday Lectionary and Jewish-Christian Relations," *Studies in Christian-Jewish Relations* 1 (2005–6): 89–102.

24. In a 2006 survey of Presbyterian Church (USA) pastors, 61% reported using the lectionary "always" or "often." See "Bible Reading in Worship Services,"

how the lectionary shapes Isaiah's role in the season of Advent continues unchanged. To use the lectionary responsibly, we must give attention to the ways the lectionary interprets Isaiah via its placement alongside specific other readings from the Gospels and Epistles and its placement within the sequence of weekly readings during Advent.

The following table lists Isaiah passages read on various days of Advent and Christmas:

Isaiah 2:1–5	First Sunday of Advent, Year A
Isaiah 7:10–16	Fourth Sunday of Advent, Year A
Isaiah 9:2–7	Nativity of the Lord–Proper I, Years A, B, C
Isaiah 11:1–10	Second Sunday of Advent, Year A
Isaiah 35:1–10	Third Sunday of Advent, Year A
Isaiah 40:1–11	Second Sunday of Advent, Year B
Isaiah 52:7–10	Nativity of the Lord–Proper III, Years A, B, C
Isaiah 61:1–4, 8–11	Third Sunday of Advent, Year B
Isaiah 61:10–62:3	First Sunday after Christmas Day, Year B
Isaiah 62:6–12	Nativity of the Lord–Proper II, Years A, B, C
Isaiah 63:7–9	First Sunday after Christmas Day, Year A
Isaiah 64:1–9	First Sunday of Advent, Year B

The next table takes a more liturgical approach to the same information.[25]

YEAR A

First Sunday of Advent	Isaiah 2:1–5
Second Sunday of Advent	Isaiah 11:1–10

The Presbyterian Panel, A Ministry of the General Assembly Council Research Services, Presbyterian Church (USA), 2006 (www.pcusa.org/research/panel). I surmise that the growth of lectionary preaching resources since this survey may lead to a higher percentage now. According to another survey, Episcopal, Lutheran (ELCA), United Methodist, and United Church of Christ (UCC) churches use the lectionary at even higher rates. See "Use of Scripture Texts from the Lectionary in Preaching," Leader Survey of the US Congregational Life Survey, April 2001 (www.USCongregations.org).

25. Only a portion of these Isaiah texts are discussed in this book.

Third Sunday of Advent	Isaiah 35:1–10
Fourth Sunday of Advent	Isaiah 7:10–16
Nativity of the Lord–Proper I	Isaiah 9:2–7
Nativity of the Lord–Proper II	Isaiah 62:6–12
Nativity of the Lord–Proper III	Isaiah 52:7–10
First Sunday after Christmas Day	Isaiah 63:7–9

Year B

First Sunday of Advent	Isaiah 64:1–9
Second Sunday of Advent	Isaiah 40:1–11
Third Sunday of Advent	Isaiah 61:1–4, 8–11
Nativity of the Lord–Proper I	Isaiah 9:2–7
Nativity of the Lord–Proper II	Isaiah 62:6–12
Nativity of the Lord–Proper III	Isaiah 52:7–10
First Sunday after Christmas Day	Isaiah 61:10–62:3

Year C

Nativity of the Lord–Proper I	Isaiah 9:2–7
Nativity of the Lord–Proper II	Isaiah 62:6–12
Nativity of the Lord–Proper III	Isaiah 52:7–10

Notice the patterns in how Isaiah is presented in the lectionary cycle. First, as the introduction to the Revised Common Lectionary states, "The structure of the Christmas cycle presumes an Advent that is basically eschatological (looking forward to the return or second coming of the Lord Jesus and the realization of the reign of God) more than a season of preparation for Christmas (which recalls his first coming among us)."[26] So, while Advent as a season carries both themes, the Revised Common Lectionary's Scripture selections seem to lean in one direction. As noted above, this confluence of multiple

26. Introduction to the Revised Common Lectionary, http://www.common texts.org/rcl, paragraph 27.

thematic elements creates some tension within worship contexts. Congregants have the events of Christmas on their minds during December as our churches are bedecked in Christmas décor and American culture pressures us to begin Christmas gift-buying even before Thanksgiving. Yet, the lectionary lessons frequently do not coincide with these elements. They bid us ponder the end of the world!

Second, the Revised Common Lectionary selects the Old Testament reading to complement the Gospel reading. In Latin this phenomenon is called *lectio selecta*. The Gospel reading is selected first, followed by the selection of the Old Testament reading. Perhaps this is a valid way to construct a table of readings, but the theological ramifications should be noted nonetheless: the reading from the Gospel takes priority and helps the lectionary creators find an appropriate selection from the Old Testament. The conversation between the two testaments thus has a dominant voice, the Gospel reading. When the search for an Old Testament passage to read during Advent begins, the Gospel reading is already affecting the choice.

Third, no matter the influence of the Gospel reading, when those in the pews see Advent as a seasonal precursor to Christmas, the season's expectation of Christ's birth significantly influences how we read the lessons from Isaiah. Isaiah is set up to play the role of an announcer or, more aptly, the predictor of this birth. Though the intent of the lectionary might be to highlight other theological themes, our cultural context, as well as the setup of the liturgical year itself, influences how the selections from Isaiah are read.

Ultimately, the Revised Common Lectionary provides a very particular and inherently limited viewpoint into Advent. Churches that use this schedule of lessons must be intentional in shaping their liturgical and homiletical approach to various Christian seasons. In the readings of Isaiah presented in the following chapters, I will pay close attention to the ways the lectionary lessons for each Sunday influence how the Isaiah passages are read and understood. A specific Gospel lesson can have an enormous effect on how a selected Isaiah passage is presented. A lectionary should be a starting place for our deliberations about preaching and reading Scripture in worship services, but we should also feel free to deviate from the lectionary to accomplish our worship plans. There is freedom to select other readings, from either testament, to present alongside the primary lesson for each Sunday.

Finally, I chose to focus in this book on the Isaiah passages that occur in the Revised Common Lectionary for Advent based on their profound association with the season and not merely because they are a part of this lectionary. Christian leaders who stand in traditions that do not use the Revised Common Lectionary will notice how these Isaiah passages are also used in liturgy, prayers, hymns, and art during Advent.

Reframing Prophecy

> Isaiah 'twas foretold it, the rose I have in mind;
> With Mary we behold it, the virgin mother kind.
> To show God's love aright
> She bore for us a savior
> When half spent was the night.[27]

The lyrics above are from the Christmas carol "Lo, How a Rose E'er Blooming." The rose referred to in this carol represents Jesus. The imagery is lovely, but let me draw your attention to the way the carol understands Isaiah's role in presenting Jesus, represented by the rose, to the world. While Mary bore him, Isaiah foretold the birth. The prophet received a prophecy that is understood in the carol as a foretelling, a prediction. It is a standard reading of the biblical prophetic literature to see in it a collection of predictions; in fact, it is so common a reading that prophecy has been taken as equivalent to a prediction.

Consequently, when Christian leaders read Isaiah during Advent, they naturally approach it as a book of future-telling. Isaiah, as a prophetic book of the Old Testament, points to the events in Jesus's

---

27. "Lo, How a Rose E'er Blooming," (no. 129) in *Glory to God: The Presbyterian Hymnal* (Louisville: Westminster John Knox, 2013). This text comprises the second verse of the hymn, which was first published in German as *Es ist ein Ros* in the fifteenth century and translated more recently by Theodore Baker.

life as recorded in the New Testament, events that were still centuries into the future. Prophecy becomes synonymous with telling the (distant) future, so Isaiah's words relate better to a time in the future and not to the prophet's present situation. For example, a preacher might note that the prophecy in Isaiah 7 was the foretelling of Jesus's birth when it mentioned the birth of a son from a "virgin" (as some translations render it). In this interpretation, the preacher claims Isaiah had divine foreknowledge of the peculiar aspects of a birth to occur several hundred years in the future.

These types of readings engage in problematic understandings of prophecy and related topics. Just consider some of the historical problems with this way of reading prophecy: First, the type of prophecy found in the book of Isaiah, considered ancient Near Eastern prophecy, was not primarily about telling the future. The prophets of ancient Israel (and ancient Mesopotamia) did not see their sole activity as foretelling. They were also "forthtellers," speaking to the religious and political issues of their day with courage and strength.[28] As mediators between God and the people, prophets delivered messages, oracles, and visions to audiences that included kings and commoners. They interpreted the past, analyzed the present, and spoke of the future but were undoubtedly more concerned with events of the present than events several hundred years in the making.[29] The carol "Lo, How a Rose E'er Blooming" may represent the state of biblical scholarship in sixteenth-century Germany, the place of its origin, but it no longer fits with current scholarly notions of Isaiah's message.

28. The Pontifical Biblical Commission's 2001 Study on *The Jewish People and Their Sacred Scriptures in the Christian Bible*, II, A, 5, §21, notes, "The original task of the prophet was to help his contemporaries understand the events and the times they lived in from God's viewpoint. Accordingly, excessive insistence, characteristic of a certain apologetic, on the probative value attributable to the fulfillment of prophecy must be discarded. This insistence has contributed to harsh judgments by Christians of Jews and their reading of the Old Testament: the more reference to Christ is found in Old Testament texts, the more the incredulity of the Jews is considered inexcusable and obstinate." http://www.vatican.va/roman_curia/congregations/cfaith/pcb_documents /rc_con_cfaith_doc_20020212_popolo-ebraico_en.html.

29. For a helpful introduction to the prophets, see Paul L. Redditt, *Introduction to the Prophets* (Grand Rapids: Eerdmans, 2008).

Another problem arises when considering why an ancient audience would take the claims of Isaiah seriously if these claims were not relevant to them, claims which would be realized and understood only hundreds of years in the future. In other words, the notion of prophecy as foretelling renders the prophet's words irrelevant to, and uninspired for, the first hearers and readers of these messages. The ancient people listened to prophets because they claimed to speak a message from God that held significance for these people in their time and place.

An additional problem with these types of readings is the notion of a messianic figure. Scholars are not convinced that the concept of such a figure was present during Isaiah's time. It is likely a later development of Second Temple Judaism, occurring after the book of Isaiah was written. This traditional Christian understanding of prophecy reads Isaiah with a slight fixation on messiah, a retroactive reading, making us find the concept in texts that may not have shared our ideas and concepts about such a figure. We think we know what we will find before we look.

These historical problems highlight the importance of historical contexts for reading biblical texts. Historical contexts help us envision the environments from which these sacred texts emerge. They offer perspective on the lives of the authors. Even for those of us who do not think the meaning of a text begins and ends with the author's intent, we must still struggle with the historical reality that the text did have meaning for the original audience (even if we can't recover it clearly), and for it to be preserved through the generations it must have continued to have new meaning. To understand how God acted in relation to humanity and the world in the past, a claim we surely want to affirm, we must pay attention to Isaiah's words as they fit into his world. Ancient contexts provide a sense that we are not the first readers of the biblical texts. They were not written primarily for us but are ancient works for ancient communities, written in an ancient language, using ancient notions of theology, biology, cosmology, and the like. Given our often overfamiliarity with these sacred texts, ancient contexts provide distance for us and help us see their strangeness again. We begin to realize our situatedness in history.

If we immediately assume Isaiah's words are a prophecy about events that will only come to pass in seven hundred years, then we forget how those same words were powerful exhortations to Isaiah's original community of readers. The reason these words were preserved through the centuries was not that readers found them unintelligible but assumed they would become evident at a future point in time; the faithful found in Isaiah's words a message for them in their context. Tying the meaning of Isaiah's words solely to the context of Jesus's life robs earlier generations of their engagement with the text.

We need not idolize an original meaning of the text as if this meaning trumps all others. Likewise, we should not look only to ancient contexts but consider readings from throughout the history of the text's interpretation. A conscious move toward the ancient contexts recognizes the importance of the writing, receiving, and transmitting of the biblical text in the past. The move helps us realize the text came from an older context; a biblical passage has a history, and often we can approximate that history.

It is helpful to think about multiple historical contexts for biblical texts, including Isaiah. When reading a biblical text, we should not merely concentrate on two points in time: the time it was written and our time today. Biblical texts were not read only at their point of origin and then again now by us. This would be like focusing on precisely two points in our own lives: our day of birth and the present moment. Texts in Isaiah have an entire history of interpretation, which includes the "originating" context in ancient Israel, their reuse and interpretation in Second Temple Judaism perhaps, their Christian context in which some Isaiah texts became christological, the Jewish context in which some texts became messianic, and then later Christian context, that is, when these texts were attached to Advent.

The book of Isaiah was composed by ancient Israelites over several centuries, from the eighth to the fifth centuries BCE. These authors wrote for their ancient Israelite audiences with no comprehension of later events such as the life of Jesus and the growth of Christianity. Thus, the book of Isaiah does not predict the birth of Jesus. Responsible and good Christian readings of the book demand more than this simplistic hermeneutic. We must acquaint ourselves with the ancient historical and social contexts that give rise to the book even as we train our eyes to other historical periods such as Jesus's own time and teachings, earliest Christianity, and our own contemporary society.

Of course, we must confess the limitations of historically contextualized readings of Isaiah. These readings ultimately do not answer our most profound theological questions because they primarily focus on historical matters. An awareness of ancient Israelite understandings of prophecy is helpful, but we do not live in ancient Israel. Discerning the historical moment when Christians began to interpret a text to be about Jesus is a worthwhile and fascinating task (especially for history buffs), but it does not speak ultimately to how Christians today should interpret the text.

We need a new sense of prophecy, a new understanding of the prophet's task. The prophets of the Hebrew Bible called their audience to respond to God's work of peace and justice. They railed against the idolatry present in their societies. They gave political advice to rulers and spiritual advice to followers without delineating between the two. They spoke a word from God into their communities. Ultimately, they are relevant to our concerns even without the notion of future-telling.

Conclusion

This initial chapter has raised questions about our near vision as Christians and the ways we read Isaiah within the Christian liturgical season of Advent. In order to develop a Christian liturgical hermeneutics, the chapter focuses on four topics. First, Advent's theological framework needs to be broadened beyond the current two theological emphases, primarily as those two themes are related almost exclusively to christological concerns. Second, Advent provides us with an opportunity to reexamine the relationship between the Hebrew Scriptures and the New Testament. Third, knowledge about the Revised Common Lectionary's use of Isaiah during Advent provides a helpful introduction to the way contemporary liturgical impulses are shaping this biblical book. And fourth, rethinking the traditional Christian notion of prophecy helps us accept ancient Israelite prophets as interpreters of their historical situations and not predictors of the distant future.

To explore our near vision, I suggested the lens of Christian liturgical hermeneutics—the notion that Christian readings of the Old Testament (and the New Testament) take the liturgical season seriously as an appropriate hermeneutical context. This type of interpretive work reflects the central role of the Bible in Christian liturgy. In fact, liturgical hermeneutics of the Bible highlights the vital relationship between the Bible and Christian worship. Gordon Lathrop notes,

> This important relationship may be seen, first of all, in the simple fact that for the vast majority of people who regard themselves as Christian a primary encounter with the actual text of the Bible comes when they go to church, comes in one of those public rituals. This was certainly true in the long history of Christianity, when Bibles or even parts of the Bible were expensive and mostly kept and owned as communal books. But it remains true today, in an age of privately owned Bibles and easily accessible electronic texts.[30]

The lens of liturgical shaping of Bible passages is one helpful way to read the Old Testament faithfully as a Christian.

30. Lathrop, *Saving Images*, 2–3.

TWO

Using Our Far Vision to Love
Our Jewish Neighbors

*We believe that revising Christian teaching about Judaism
and the Jewish people is a central and indispensable obligation of theology in our time. It is essential that Christianity both understand and represent Judaism accurately, not
only as a matter of justice for the Jewish people, but also for
the integrity of Christian faith, which we cannot proclaim
without reference to Judaism.*

"A Sacred Obligation: Rethinking Christian Faith
in Relation to Judaism and the Jewish People"

When we proclaim Isaiah in our churches, we have the opportunity
to acknowledge that we share this biblical book with another religious tradition, Judaism. When reading from Isaiah, we might explicitly state this fact: "Isaiah is not just a part of Christian Scripture; it
is also a prophetic book within the Jewish Bible" or "Today we hear
words from a book held sacred by both Jews and Christians." This
simple and accurate statement holds enormous ethical import as it
compels us to recognize our religious neighbors even as we worship.
Naming our shared reliance on Isaiah is a good first step, but we can
go further. We might commit to a Christian interpretation of Isaiah
that does not exclude Jewish interpretations: "As Christians, we understand Isaiah through our histories and theologies, but Jews do not
read Isaiah this way." An excellent second step. Statements like this
affirm the integrity of each religious tradition as it struggles to interpret its sacred Scripture. However, this statement does not address
how certain interpretations within one religious tradition might

cause harm to another tradition. So we might go a step further and commit to a Christian interpretation that has no potential for harm to Jews, an interpretation that does not portray them in a negative light. In other words, we are neighborly; we share as good neighbors. This chapter discusses in depth the third and most difficult step as a way forward toward love and concern for our Jewish neighbors. As the opening quotation to this chapter clearly states, we must revise our Christian proclamation to "understand and represent Judaism accurately." We need to attend to our "far vision" to look beyond our tradition and how it might affect others.

I deliberately use the concept *neighbor* to express the Christian's attitude toward, and regard for, Jews. Love of neighbor is central to both faith traditions. The command to love your neighbor is given in Leviticus 19:18 and is used in both Judaism and Christianity as a crucial element of ethics. As Christians, we take Jesus's response to a question regarding the heart of the Jewish Torah seriously: *You shall love God with all your being and love your neighbor as yourself* (Mark 12:28–34). Therefore, we also apply this ethical standard to our interpretations of the Bible: Does this reading of Scripture help us love our neighbor? If a particular reading of Scripture leads us to think badly of Jews, then is this reading Christian? When we love our neighbors, we show great concern for them; we attempt not to harm them. An ethic of neighborly love allows us to make judgments about certain interpretations of biblical texts.

I also use the concept of *neighbor* because neighbors do not always agree. In fact, they sometimes disagree and have to take seriously one another's perceptions, feelings, and opinions. Being neighborly is being attentive and listening well to the concerns of others. It is realizing that your actions affect those around you. Christians act neighborly when they take seriously Jewish critiques of Christianity and Christian teachings, just as Jews act neighborly when they offer these critiques. For example, one serious question debated in Jewish-Christian relations is whether the New Testament is inherently anti-Jewish. One particular answer to that question is formed by Elizabeth Berkovitz, an Orthodox Jewish philosopher who writes about the Holocaust:

Christianity's New Testament has been the most dangerous anti-Semitic tract in history. Its hatred-charged diatribes against the "Pharisees" and the Jews have poisoned the hearts and minds of millions and millions of Christians for almost two millennia now. . . . No matter what the deeper theological meaning of the hate passages against the Jews might be, in the history of the Jewish people the New Testament lent its inspiring support to oppression, persecution and mass murder of an intensity and duration that were unparalleled in the entire history of man's degradation. Without Christianity's New Testament, Hitler's *Mein Kampf* could never have been written.[1]

As a Christian, I find this a difficult but neighborly word. It is challenging and jarring to hear the New Testament linked so directly to Hitler. It is a challenge from our neighbor that we need to ponder. It is an essential reminder that neighbors often speak uncomfortable truths to us and help us see a different perspective.

As I participate in my local congregation and visit other churches during the season of Advent, I am bothered by the ways we fail to share Isaiah as good neighbors. We do not use the book of Isaiah as an instrument of force against our neighbors, nor do I hear insulting remarks about Jews—ancient or contemporary—in modern pulpits and lecterns.[2] Our unneighborly behavior is more subtle than using Isaiah to make disparaging remarks about Jews (or Muslims).[3] Our use of Isaiah is more along the lines of viewing him as a Christian, as if the book has no authority in Judaism and his words are for our benefit alone. This treatment is unintentional, and indeed it is not malicious. These types of potentially harmful interpretations are nearsightedness, myopia. We are so focused on

1. Elizabeth Berkovitz, "Facing the Truth," *Judaism* 27 (1978): 324–26, here 324–25.

2. We might need to make an exception to this statement for the Pharisees, because we do hear negative comments about them regularly. But there are no Pharisees in Isaiah so it is not necessary to broach this issue here.

3. However, we Christians have certainly participated in this type of polemic during our history.

the objects near us that other religious traditions are blurry. Consider what would happen if we moved away from these patterns toward more intentional and reflective readings of Isaiah. What issues must we face and teachings must we revise in order to share as neighbors and constructively create helpful boundaries between our geographies while yet sharing a fence? We are capable of creating a more robust understanding of Advent and readings from Isaiah as we engage these questions. Indeed we are capable of using the season of Advent to draw nearer to Judaism by attending to the prophetic tradition we share.

Three issues are at play in Christians' ability to read the book of Isaiah during Advent while loving our neighbor and upholding the validity and vibrancy of Judaism. There are matters of history, problematic theology, and ethical stance to consider. The historical matter involves our inattention to scholarly notions of messiah and the critical need to reexamine Second Temple Judaism's (515 BCE–70 CE) and early Christianity's concepts of messiah. The theological problem relates to our supersessionist tendencies whereby we often portray Christianity and the church as the natural successor to ancient Israel. In this reading, Judaism is brushed aside as unimportant because it represents a divergence from the witness of the Old Testament. Our ethical stance relates to the impact our Christian interpretations of Isaiah have on people, namely, Jews. We fail to realize how our interpretations negatively portray the Jews, or we forget that their interpretations have merit.

The Messiah

For Christians, claiming Jesus as the Messiah is often presumed. Even though it is a foundational notion within Christianity, the topic of messiah is complex and open to interpretation from a historical perspective. Scholars of Second Temple Judaism and its literature have more questions than definite answers. We do not need to explore the concept's development, from its roots in Old Testament notions of kingship through Second Temple Jewish texts such as the Dead Sea Scrolls to New Testament texts, to appreciate some of the essential findings of contemporary biblical scholarship.[4] Instead, we focus on messiah only as it relates to sharing Isaiah with our Jewish neighbors. Does Isaiah have a notion of a messiah? Does the claim that Jesus is the Messiah help us love our neighbor? What are the theological and interfaith implications of messiah for Christian-Jewish relations?

We speak of "Jesus Christ" with "Christ" being the corresponding Greek title for the Hebrew word *messiah*. The Pauline corpus uses the Greek word *christos* over two hundred fifty times for Jesus.[5] However, what is a messiah? A Christ? How do we know one when we see one? In Hebrew, *messiah* has the basic meaning of "anointed." It is used in the Old Testament about several individuals, including King David and the Persian ruler Cyrus. However, we do not consider either of these leaders to be messiahs. Why? Because the word accumulates meaning in the Second Temple period so that eventually "an anointed one" has other connotations. John J. Collins helpfully explains that, although the Hebrew word can mean "anointed," we should, at a minimum, reserve the term *messiah* for an eschatological figure.[6] This figure could take the form of a king, priest, prophet, or heavenly messiah, but is linked to end times. In other words, the concept of a messiah undergoes a development: it begins as a Hebrew word to describe an anointed person as one example, but eventually it develops into a more robust concept associated with the end of time.

Confusion regarding this historical development sometimes leads to notions of messiah in the Old Testament that are, in fact, not historically accurate to the period when the passage was written. We are encouraged to read the Old Testament this way by authors such as Matthew, who explicitly use the Old Testament to make connections between Jesus and Matthew's Jewish audience. We should pause here to rehearse that biblical passages have meanings beyond those

---

4. The best resource for this sort of scholarly tour through the literature remains John J. Collins, *The Scepter and the Star: The Messiahs of the Dead Sea Scrolls and Other Ancient Literature*, Anchor Bible Reference Library (New York: Doubleday, 1995); concerning the question of messiah within the Hebrew Bible only, see Ronald E. Clements, "The Messianic Hope in the Old Testament," *Journal for the Study of the Old Testament* 43 (1989): 3–19.

5. Collins, *Scepter and Star*, 2.

6. Collins, *Scepter and Star*, 11–12.

ascribed to them at their origins. Texts are not bound by their origins. Our readings of biblical passages change as contexts change. So we are not trying to disregard Christian interpretations of Isaiah that find a messianic figure. We are, however, noting that in contemporary historical scholarship on the Bible, we now know that Isaiah, a book written during the eighth to fifth centuries BCE, would not have had a concept of messiah as it is later sketched out in Second Temple Judaism. Just as contemporary Christians have to rethink our understandings of creation in light of our knowledge of evolution, we also have to rethink our understandings of Isaiah in light of our knowledge of the history of ideas.

Isaiah, then, contains some passages, such as chapter 9, that participate in a royal ideology where the king is envisioned as the son of God by adoption:

> For a child has been born to us, a son given to us;
> dominion was upon his shoulders;
> his name was called Wonderful Counselor, Mighty God,
>   Father Evermore, Chief of Peace.
> There will be no end to the abundance of his reign and to
>   peace concerning the throne of David and his king-
>   dom, to prepare it and to support it with justice and
>   righteousness from now until forever. The zeal of The
>   Living God of hosts will do this. (Isaiah 9:6–7)

The royal figure is extraordinary but not divine. The birth and reign are presented within a clear historical context, not an eschatological one. Isaiah 11, then, displays hope for a Davidic leader, an ideal king, who will reign in history (as opposed to at the end of time):

> But a branch will come forth from a stump of Jesse,
> and a sprout from his roots will bear fruit.
> The spirit of The Living God will rest upon him—
> a spirit of wisdom and understanding,
> a spirit of advice and determination,
> a spirit of knowledge and fear of The Living God—
> and his delight will be in the fear of The Living God.

> He will not judge according to the appearance of his eyes;
> and he will not mediate according to the rumor of his ears.
> But he will judge with justice the helpless poor,
> and mediate with fairness the needy of the earth.
> He will strike the earth with the rod of his mouth,
> and with the breath of his lips, he will kill the wicked.
> Justice will be the waistcloth of his hips,
> and faithfulness the waistcloth of his loins. (Isaiah 11:1–5)

These two Isaiah passages and others will be taken up in later periods and read through a messianic lens. Jews and Christians share this rich theological tradition, one that dares to imagine a new way of governance, a new kingdom.

Notions of a messiah developed considerably during the middle and late Second Temple Period, that is, after most of the Hebrew Bible was written. For example, the Dead Sea Scrolls mention messianic or eschatological figures. By the time of the arrival of Jesus during the first century CE, Judaism holds a belief in the expectation of a Davidic messiah.[7] There was serious diversity of thought surrounding the notion, including talk of a warrior king and priest figure as well as a messianic prophet modeled on Isaiah 61.[8]

Now that we have seen the historical elements of messianism, it is essential to say a few words about theological implications. Gershom Scholem begins his scholarly work on messianism with the following helpful, if overly generalized, comment: "Any discussion of the problems relating to Messianism is a delicate matter, for it is here that the essential conflict between Judaism and Christianity has developed and continues to exist."[9] Indeed, Jews and Christians are divided, or in conflict, over the idea of messiah. What one tradition

---

7. Collins, *Scepter and Star*, 49, 74.

8. John J. Collins, *The Apocalyptic Imagination*, 2nd edition (Grand Rapids: Eerdmans, 1998), 263; Matthew V. Novenson, *Christ among the Messiahs: Christ Language in Paul and Messiah Language in Ancient Judaism* (Oxford: Oxford University Press, 2015); Matthew V. Novenson, *The Grammar of Messianism: An Ancient Jewish Political Idiom and Its Users* (Oxford: Oxford University Press, 2016).

9. Gershom Scholem, *The Messianic Idea in Judaism and Other Essays on*

claims as central, the other utterly rejects; Jesus as the Christ is so central to Christianity that a denunciation of this claim by Jews has led to Christian persecution of Jews.

So, how do we, as Christians, continue to affirm one of our central claims of Jesus as the Messiah while also allowing space for the dismissal of that claim? Perhaps we are helped by returning to the tension between identity and openness. Christians maintain strong identities in the claim of Jesus as the Christ while also remaining open to other visions of the messianic kingdom, thus realizing that the full realm of God has not come. It is vital to our identity to claim Jesus as the Messiah, and we are also open to other formulations of messiah.

One meaningful way forward along this challenging path is not to claim too much: to be careful, considerate, and humble with our messianic notions. For example, instead of holding to a messianic or christological reading of Isaiah as the only valid notion, Christians could admit openly and explicitly that these texts provide some of the necessary elements that will constitute notions of messiahship in first-century Judaism, notions Jesus and his biographers took up and used. However, these texts do not point immediately to Jesus; there is just not a straight line—historically or theologically— between Point A, Isaiah, and Point B, Jesus. This sort of admission presents real possibilities for neighborly engagement since it ties the Christian claim about Jesus more closely to sacred texts that are used only by Christians. It does not predetermine the meaning of Isaiah for all traditions, but it allows Jews and Christians to interpret Isaiah's prophecies based on their respective traditions, with neither tradition holding ultimate authority over the biblical text. This approach aligns with recent Christian teaching by the Roman Catholic Church: "The Jewish reading of the Bible is a possible one, in continuity with the Jewish Sacred Scriptures [, . . .] a reading analogous to the Christian reading which developed in parallel fashion."[10] We could go even further to say that the Jewish reading is an important and necessary one from which Christians could learn.

Jewish Spirituality (New York: Schocken, 1971), 1. Quoted in Collins, *Scepter and Star*, 1.

10. *The Jewish People and Their Sacred Scriptures in the Christian Bible,* II, A, 7, §22.

Also, Christians can proclaim that even though the Messiah has come, we wait with Jews for the "complete realization of the messianic age."[11] So, "it is the mission of the Church, as also that of the Jewish people, to proclaim and to work to prepare the world for the full flowering of God's Reign, which is, but is 'not yet.'"[12] This quote is an Advent claim. It makes room for our longing concerning the fullness of God's dream for our world. It takes the unique identity of Christians seriously as ones who have seen in Jesus our Messiah yet remain open to the fullness of that claim in the future.

Supersessionism

In our coexistence with Jews over the centuries, Christians have invalidated Judaism by portraying it as inferior to our faith. In many cases, this invalidation was intentional and malicious; we tried to distinguish our faith from Judaism by deriding the religion. We claimed we had replaced Judaism with the development of a better religion and improved way of faith. We claimed that the church had replaced or superseded the Jewish people as God's people.[13] This train of thought harkens to the second century CE and Justin Martyr, who falsely claimed God rejected Israel as the chosen people, replacing them with the Christian church.[14] This sentiment, and others like it, continued unabated into the twentieth century. One can see such Christian disregard for the Jewish people as a contributing factor to the Holocaust.[15]

Fortunately, we are learning—slowly—a new way forward.

In light of horrific past events such as the Holocaust and more

---

11. Mary Boys, *Has God Only One Blessing? Judaism as a Source of Christian Self-Understanding* (New York: Paulist, 2000), 287.

12. Boys, *Has God Only One Blessing?*, 287.

13. Supersessionism is sometimes called "replacement theology." See Edward Kessler, *An Introduction to Jewish-Christian Relations* (Cambridge: Cambridge University Press, 2010), 170–79.

14. Justin Martyr, *Dialogue with Trypho*, 119.1–5.

15. Robert Ericksen, *Complicity in the Holocaust: Churches and Universities in Nazi Germany* (Cambridge: Cambridge University Press, 2012).

frequent day-to-day interactions with Jews in our religiously diverse world, we see the mistakes of an exclusive faith, a faith that claims to be the true replacement to another religion. Many Christian denominations have issued statements in the last few decades, renewing commitments to Jewish-Christian dialogue, interfaith work, and mutual learning and understanding.[16] Within the larger picture of religious pluralism, Christians have increasingly begun to identify as pluralists.[17]

Christian invalidation of Judaism is often unintentional and unplanned as it has remained embedded and unexplored in our theologies and litanies. Although we no longer seek to portray Christianity as a replacement to Judaism, nor do we honestly believe such a notion, we still unknowingly or inadvertently proclaim that message through the ways we talk about Christianity. We admire Judaism but then turn to proclaim a supersessionist vision of Christianity.

We have participated too often in supersessionism. We share many theological values and ideas with Judaism, but supersessionism goes beyond our commonly held beliefs. Susannah Heschel defines supersessionism as follows:

> The appropriation by the New Testament and the early church of Judaism's central theological teachings, including messiah, eschatology, apocalypticism, election, and Israel, as well as its scriptures, its prophets, and even its God, while denying the continued validity of those teachings and texts within Judaism as an independent path to salvation.[18]

This definition emphasizes how Christianity both shares various theological concepts with Judaism—in fact, Heschel uses the stronger language of appropriation—yet denies Judaism the ability to use those same concepts. Supersessionism is a theological colonization of Judaism.[19]

---

16. http://www.ccjr.us/dialogika-resources/documents-and-statements.

17. Paul F. Knitter, *Introducing Theologies of Religions* (Maryknoll, NY: Orbis, 2002).

18. Susannah Heschel, *The Aryan Jesus: Christian Theologians and the Bible in Nazi Germany* (Princeton: Princeton University Press, 2008), 26.

19. Heschel, *Aryan Jesus*, 27.

This appropriation and denial, while certainly having its origins in the New Testament and early church, continues today. The early church was not the only offender. Christians have assumed many theological themes and Scripture passages without noting how these themes and passages have validity and importance in Judaism. The borrowing and adapting of certain teachings are acceptable. Religious reformers are always adapting traditions and creating new ones. Furthermore, Judaism and Christianity grew out of the same milieu. They are siblings. Supersessionism occurs when one religious tradition, in this case, Christianity, begins to think of itself as having taken the place of the other tradition, Judaism. To supersede is to supplant.

Instead of seeing how these two ancient religions distinctly deal with various theological points, supersessionism elevates one while simultaneously invalidating the other. As Rolf Rendtorff notes,

> The crucial point is the theological acceptance or, first of all, even awareness, of the existence of contemporary Judaism as a living religion which uses the Hebrew Bible as its Holy Scripture. Christian theologians, Old Testament scholars included, have never been taught to realize that. I myself during more than ten years of teaching Old Testament was never aware of this problem. As far as I can see, there are still very few Christian biblical scholars who are aware of all this.[20]

If scholars are not aware, then who can blame educated clergy for not paying closer attention to this crucial ethical issue? Hopefully, we have made some progress since this observation was written.

To move away from supersessionist thinking, we need to develop reading strategies that align with theological statements such as these:

> For centuries Christians claimed that their covenant with God replaced or superseded the Jewish covenant. We renounce this claim. We believe that God does not revoke divine promises. We affirm

20. Rolf Rendtorff, *Canon and Theology* (Minneapolis: Fortress, 1993), 43.

that God is in covenant with both Jews and Christians. . . . Our recognition of the abiding validity of Judaism has implications for all aspects of Christian life.[21]

Such statements can help us read anew and share our Scriptures. They help us frame discussions of covenant differently and give us the courage to state forthrightly that God is indeed in covenant with Jews. God is a promise keeper! Jews are a part of the covenant.

While we may not state forthrightly such a version of supersessionism (for example, the covenant with the Jews is no longer valid), it is tempting when approaching the Bible to glide smoothly into a reading of Isaiah that portrays Christianity as the natural successor to, or replacement of, Judaism. In our faith's early history, it may have been a deliberate move of identity formation and polemic to think of Christianity as superseding Judaism, yet now it is uncommon to think in these explicit terms about our neighbors. Furthermore, we usually associate supersessionist readings with the New Testament because it is in those biblical texts that the emerging relationship between the two "religions" is beginning to be worked out.

Our newer understandings of the relationship between Judaism and Christianity, including the vital notion that Judaism remains a vibrant religion, have not wholly affected the way we read and hear biblical texts. The tendency is to think of our spiritual history as developing through Abraham and Sarah, Moses and his sister Miriam, and David straight into the New Testament of Jesus, Paul, and Peter without realizing we share much of that history with contemporary Judaism.

Theological and ethical dangers exist when one chooses a piece of sacred literature shared by more than one religious tradition and reads it through the lens of a single tradition. Christian readings, standing firmly and faithfully within their tradition, may produce helpful interpretations for that tradition while doing no harm to

---

21. Mary C. Boys, ed., *Seeing Judaism Anew: Christianity's Sacred Obligation* (Lanham, MD: Rowman and Littlefield, 2005), xiv. This quotation is taken from a larger statement by the Christian Scholars Group on Christian-Jewish Relations.

Judaism. However, if the tradition is not diligent, some readings may ignore the presence of Judaism or assume to be the only tradition reading these particular books. Judaism as a vibrant tradition can be a force to help us with our parochialism and provincialism.[22]

In the previous chapter, we considered the unhelpful prophecy-fulfillment paradigm. At this point, we can see how such a paradigm can lead to supersessionism. When Christians view the stories from the Old Testament as issuing a promise that needs the New Testament, especially the words and actions of Jesus, in order to fulfill the promise, it becomes difficult for the Old Testament to speak to Christians as an authoritative text for the life of the faith community. It assumes the Old Testament is incomplete and needs something else to become whole.[23] It assumes the words of the Old Testament cannot stand alone as a witness to the actions and ways of God, when in fact, this canon does stand without the New Testament for our Jewish neighbors. For example, in a book about preaching the Old Testament, I recently read the following assertion: "The Old Testament is incomplete without the New, a single redemptive history is the river that holds the Old and New Testament together, the person of Jesus Christ unites the two Testaments."[24] All three of these thoughts are problematic insofar as they do not consider the existence and continued validity of contemporary Judaism. First, for Jews, the Old Testament, which they call the Tanakh or Mikra, is complete. Even for Christians, the Old Testament can stand alone as a faithful witness to God. Second, the author's assertion of a single redemptive history blatantly ignores the redemptive history of ancient Israel, which is also claimed by rabbinic Judaism resulting in our modern denominations of Judaism. Third, the claim that Jesus unites the testaments imposes a single hermeneutic for a large and

22. Marianne Moyaert, *Fragile Identities: Towards a Theology of Interreligious Hospitality* (Amsterdam: Rodopi, 2011), 70; Paul F. Knitter, *One Earth, Many Religions: Multifaith Dialogue and Global Responsibility* (Maryknoll, NY: Orbis, 1995), 456.

23. A parallel error occurs when Christians call Jewish converts to Christianity "completed Jews."

24. Sidney Greidanus, *Preaching Christ from the Old Testament: A Contemporary Hermeneutical Method* (Grand Rapids: Eerdmans, 1999), 51.

diverse collection of books. Finally, the Hebrew Scriptures contain several stories in which God has redeemed the people (for example, the exodus from Egypt). Thus, the Old Testament is not the story of a people who just kept waiting for redemption; instead, it is a story of a people who were redeemed again and again.

Another example comes from a prominent twentieth-century Old Testament scholar, Martin Noth, who observed, "Jesus himself, with his words and his work, no longer formed part of the history of Israel. In him the history of Israel had come, rather, to its real end."[25] In other words, according to Noth, Jesus marks the end of Israel and the beginning of Christianity; Jesus's life stands so outside the boundaries of Judaism (or to use Noth's terminology, "the history of Israel") that he already transcends it. Noth pays no attention to Second Temple Judaism, nascent rabbinic Judaism, or his contemporary Jewish neighbors. They are ignored because Jesus is not a part of Israel, no matter how we define it.

The discussion of supersessionism leads to the thorny topic of christological interpretations of the Old Testament and specifically of Isaiah. These interpretations view the prophetic book through the lens of Christ. Typically they assert that Isaiah's primary or exclusive message relates directly to Christ. Imagine a twelfth-century Latin manuscript of Jerome's commentary on Isaiah. On the manuscript is a miniature drawing of two figures, Jerome and Isaiah, who is holding two scrolls. Jerome is looking up at Isaiah and saying: "Dic tu Isaias, dic testimonium Christi" ("Go on, Isaiah, tell them about Christ").[26] We see supersessionist tendencies in the Christian interpretive shift from Isaiah as a prophet to Isaiah as an evangelist. As an evangelist, Isaiah becomes a distinctly Christian book instead of a prophetic book for both Jews and Christians. Isaiah's original prophetic ministry and his continuing relevance to the Jewish community today are erased

25. Martin Noth, *The History of Israel,* 2nd edition (New York: Harper and Row, 1960), 432.

26. Manuscript is found in Durham Cathedral Library. The miniature is at the beginning of Book VIII (on chapters 24–27). The scrolls have Isaiah 7:14 and 24:16 on them.

when Isaiah is transformed into an evangelist. Allowing Isaiah to remain as a prophet within both the Christian and Jewish traditions leads to sharing and dialogue concerning how this figure and his book speak into these traditions.

I affirm with the United Church of Christ that "God's covenant with the Jewish people has not been rescinded or abrogated by God, but remains in full force."[27] Alternatively, to put it as the Christian Scholars Group on Christian-Jewish Relations does: "God's covenant with the Jewish people endures forever."[28] Therefore, we strive to read the Hebrew Scriptures faithfully in ways clarifying God's ongoing covenant with God's people, the Jews. We stridently avoid readings that claim God's covenant is with Christians only. Also, we avoid readings operating as if Christians have an exclusive claim on the Hebrew Bible. We share this text with Judaism; we read differently as Christians, but our readings do not have to participate in supersessionism.

Anti-Judaism

The third major issue impeding our abilities to read Isaiah during Advent is Christian anti-Judaism. Unfortunately, as we have already seen, Christianity has a long tradition of animosity toward Judaism. The *Adversus Judaeos* (Against the Jews) tradition within our faith should not be an element of pride. Indeed, we should be repentant. The teachings and ministry of Jesus did not permit us as the church to commit detrimental actions and use harmful rhetoric toward our neighbors. In fact, it is now ever more evident to us that our early, evolving, positive definitions of Christianity and church were formed

27. "Relationship between the UCC and the Jewish Community" resolution adopted by the 16th synod of the UCC in 1987. See also this thoughtful response to this resolution: Denise Dombkowski Hopkins, "God's Continuing Covenant with the Jews and the Christian Reading of the Bible," *Prism* 3, no. 2 (1988): 6–75.

28. One can find this statement in Boys, ed., *Seeing Judaism Anew*, or online: http://www.ccjr.us/dialogika-resources/documents-and-statements/ecumeni cal-christian/568-csg-02sep1.

over and against negative definitions of Judaism. This unfortunate history need not be rehearsed here, although we should unequivocally denounce it as a true expression of Jesus's teachings. We cannot erase it or dismiss it; we can only repent and condemn it.

Defining anti-Judaism is difficult. First, the term is often confused with antisemitism.[29] Most would say anti-Judaism focuses on religious aspects while antisemitism is racialist in nature. They are of course interrelated, since they target the same people. We are concerned with Christian misunderstandings, ignorance, and hatred of Jews and Judaism because of Jewish religious teachings, practices, and ethics. This type of Christian animosity to Jews dates to a period well before modern antisemitism. As Jews and Christians began to part ways in the early centuries of the Common Era, Christians, who gained power under the Roman emperor Constantine, began to mistreat and denigrate Jews. Eventually, this disdain was made official by the church and became known later as a "teaching of contempt."[30]

One facet of anti-Judaism is its assumption or confusion that ancient Israelites of the Old Testament (and ancient Judeans of the New Testament) are similar to, or identical with, contemporary Jews in religious beliefs and practices. This Christian interpretive move goes as far back in history as Justin Martyr, who applied Isaiah's prophetic judgment against the ancient Israelites to all Jews, including the Jews of his second-century CE world. This bias continues today, often because of a lack of contact between Christians and Jews. Christians, therefore, receive much of their knowledge of Jews and Judaism through reading their Bibles. Unfortunately, they are not always aware that Judaism has developed considerably over

29. *Antisemitism* as a word occurred for the first time in the late nineteenth century as racial theories began to classify people. These theories have been proven bogus and utter nonsense so that today we spell antisemitism with lower case letters in order to demonstrate its lack of validity. See Gavin I. Langmuir, *Toward a Definition of Antisemitism* (Berkeley: University of California Press, 1990).

30. Jules Isaac, a twentieth-century Jewish historian, coined the term. See his *The Teaching of Contempt: Christian Roots of Anti-Semitism*, ed. Claire Huchet-Bishop and trans. Helen Weaver (New York: Holt, Rinehart & Winston, 1964).

the past millennia. Modern Jews are not Pharisees. This statement
may seem obvious, but it is not rare to hear Christian sermons on
Gospel texts that consistently refer to first-century Jewish groups as
"Jews" without any recognition that this term is used today to refer
to our neighbors. And that two thousand years separate these two
groups. Imagine if the only knowledge you had of Christianity was
the information you gleaned about Saint Augustine from his writings
so that when you met a contemporary Christian today, you assumed
that they were identical to Augustine in belief and practice.

Today we know, as "A Sacred Obligation" states, "Judaism is a living faith, enriched by many centuries of development."[31] The Jewish
faith today as practiced and lived by around sixteen million people
does not look like the faith of the ancient Israelites. Jews no longer
sacrifice animals. They do not worship in a temple. Some Jews follow
kosher laws; others do not.

Another facet of anti-Judaism relates to negative stereotypes concerning Jewish religion. Christians often caricature Judaism as a religion of law. They often view Judaism through the lens of a particular
reading of the apostle Paul, who says, "Christ has redeemed us from
the curse of the law" (Galatians 3:13). Using this lens, Christians view
Judaism as legalistic and self-righteous in its devotion to rules. Think
of our contemporary use of the word *pharisaic* to describe people
who are moralizing and sanctimonious. In contrast to this incorrect
understanding, Judaism views itself as a religion committed to justice
and love as it is presented in their sacred texts and the traditions that
have grown up around them. To take one example, a recent book by
Jon Levenson argues that the biblical injunction to love God reveals a
profoundly special relationship between God and God's people that
is more than contractual or legalistic. Levenson speaks of the "mutual
faithfulness" existing between these two parties and of the people's
response of gratitude to God's love.[32] It is anti-Jewish to suggest this
major world religion is under "the curse of the law."

A final aspect of anti-Judaism concerns ignoring or degrading the

31. Statement online: http://www.ccjr.us/dialogika-resources/documents
-and-statements/ecumenical-christian/568-csg-02sep1.

32. Jon D. Levenson, *The Love of God: Divine Gift, Human Grati-*

tradition's own understanding of its sacred Scriptures. Our Christian reading of Isaiah is not an attempt to diminish or silence Jewish readings. We do not claim here to have any monopoly on the book. However, it is not enough to note merely the presence and even legitimacy of another faith tradition's readings; we are compelled to make sure our overtly Christian readings of the text do not lapse either explicitly or implicitly into anti-Jewish readings.

Post-Holocaust, Christian Reading

"Ask yourselves if the theology you are learning is such that it could remain unchanged before and after Auschwitz. If this be the case, be on your guard."[33] We live "post-Holocaust" or "after Auschwitz." The Holocaust exposes uniquely and undeniably Christianity's long and persistent history of anti-Judaism; the Shoah[34] graphically shows how Christianity's troublesome relationship with Judaism can be used for deadly purposes. The events of the Holocaust sharpen our ability to see how our Christian readings of the Old and New Testaments have contributed to physical and emotional harm and violence against Jews.

In light of this horrifying event, which occurred less than a century ago, we seek to change our relationship with Jews by changing our theologies, interpretations, and liturgies. We strive to act as neighbors and to align our readings of the Bible, so these readings also become an act of loving our neighbor. To read anew, in our post-

---

tude, and Mutual Faithfulness in Judaism (Princeton: Princeton University Press, 2016).

33. Johannes Baptist Metz, *The Emergent Church*, trans. Peter Mann (New York: Crossroad, 1981), 29.

34. For an exploration of the various terminology used to signify the Third Reich's murder of approximately six million Jews as well as other humans, see Richard L. Rubenstein and John K. Roth, *Approaches to Auschwitz: The Holocaust and Its Legacy* (Louisville: Westminster John Knox, 2003), 1–22; Zev Garber and Bruce Zuckerman, "Why Do We Call the Holocaust 'The Holocaust'? An Inquiry into the Psychology of Labels," *Modern Judaism* 9, no. 2 (1989): 197–211.

Holocaust world, is to accept the challenges of the previous chapter as opportunities for spiritual growth. I would go so far as to claim that these challenges highlight for us how our current readings may not be thoroughly Christian but may rely more on traditional notions concerning Judaism that we do not wish to perpetuate, outdated notions of biblical prophecy that need serious rethinking, and unhelpful paradigms of religious pluralism.

We are interested in post-Holocaust, Christian *readings* of Isaiah. I will not advocate for one Christian reading of a particular Isaiah passage; in fact, I acknowledge a variety of ways Christians can read the Old Testament distinctively while avoiding supersessionist interpretations. I agree wholeheartedly with Walter Brueggemann when he states, "For those who do interpretation—especially Christian interpretation—the Shoah stands as a dread-filled summons to unlearn a great deal. For Christians this means the unlearning of 'final readings,' for 'final readings' tend, I suggest, to give ground for 'final solutions.'"[35]

As progressive Christians move away from exclusive christological readings of Isaiah, it is tempting to retreat to the safety of historical-critical readings, which prioritize the ancient world. However, contemporary Christians (and Jews) need to relate their ancient sacred stories and literature to their current situations and lives. Must those who find christological readings of Isaiah problematic simply follow scholars' historical readings of these Isaiah texts? Are we forced as Jews and Christians to seek only historical interpretations of Isaiah to which we can both agree? What do we lose with such a narrow reading?

Conclusion

We close this chapter with an image brought to our attention by Christian theologian Mary Boys. In her work on Jewish-Christian

35. Walter Brueggemann, "A Fissure Always Uncontained," in *Strange Fire: Reading the Bible after the Holocaust*, ed. Tod Linafelt (New York: New York University Press, 2000), 62–75, here 64. See also his "Reading from the Day 'In Between,'" in *A Shadow of Glory: Reading the New Testament after the Holocaust*, ed. Tod Linafelt (New York: Routledge, 2002), 105–16.

relations, she appeals to specific medieval Christian iconography in various cathedrals visually depicting the relationship between Christianity and Judaism: "we see a triumphant Ecclesia [representing Christianity] standing erect next to the bowed, blindfolded figure of the defeated yet dignified Synagoga. . . . Though the church has triumphed over synagogue, the latter is a tragic rather than sinister figure—a woman conquered, with her crown fallen, staff broken, and Torah dropping to the ground."[36] This is undoubtedly not the way we wish to represent the relationship between Judaism and Christianity today as we have taken formal steps to change this relationship through denominational statements and interfaith cooperation. Now we follow those steps with a commitment to genuinely sharing our sacred stories in ways that enliven both traditions.

36. Boys, *Has God Only One Blessing?*, 33.

PART TWO

Isaiah's "Messianic" Texts

THREE

Isaiah 7:10–16

The Fourth Sunday of Advent in Year A

O holy Child of Bethlehem, descend to us, we pray;
Cast out our sin, and enter in, be born in us today!
We hear the Christmas angels the great glad tidings tell;
O come to us, abide with us, our Lord Emmanuel!

Phillips Brooks, "O Little Town of Bethlehem"

¹⁰ Again The Living God spoke to Ahaz: ¹¹ "Request a sign of confirmation from The Living God, your God. Make it deep like the underworld or high like the sky." ¹² And Ahaz said, "I will neither request nor test The Living God."

¹³ Then Isaiah said, "Hear, O House of David. Is it a little matter for you all to weary people that you weary also my God? ¹⁴ Therefore, my God will give you all a sign: Look! The young woman is pregnant and about to give birth to a son. She will name him With-us-is-God. ¹⁵ By the time he knows to reject evil and choose good, he will eat cream and honey. ¹⁶ Before the youth knows to reject evil and choose good, the land of the two kings whom you abhor will be abandoned."

This short passage from the larger narrative of Isaiah 7 contains the well-known story of the child named Immanuel. In this chapter, we focus on four historical contexts for understanding Isaiah 7: the eighth-century BCE context of the prophetic announcement, the first-century CE reuse of the prophecy by the Gospel of Matthew, the rabbinic understanding of the prophecy, and our contemporary context. We see the richness of this passage as it gains new interpretations in different historical contexts and as it continues to resonate during the Advent season.

The Originating Context of Isaiah 7

The first word of the first verse in this passage—"again"—alerts us to the detail that the passage does not contain the first divine message delivered to Ahaz, the king of Judah. We must begin reading earlier in the chapter. Isaiah 7:1–9 relates a prophetic announcement to King Ahaz of Judah during a particularly scary time of his reign, when the neighboring kings of Aram and Israel—both to the north of Judah—sought to attack Jerusalem, Judah's capital. These kings—Rezin of Aram/Syria/Damascus and Pekah of Israel—wanted Ahaz to ally with them against the campaigning superpower, Assyria, and they were willing to use coercion to build this crucial alliance. Some of the details of this period are found in 2 Kings 15–16 or by researching the Syro-Ephraimitic War/Crisis in scholarly resources. Isaiah was divinely commanded to take his son, whose name means "a remnant will turn back," and go to Ahaz to calm and reassure the king. Isaiah instructed Ahaz not to fear because Rezin and Pekah would not succeed in their plan. The prophetic reason for the kings' assured failure was based on Isaiah's understanding of Jerusalem and the Davidic dynasty. The prophet believed strongly that the city and the throne of David were invincible given their special status with God. Thus, the neighboring kings were doomed to failure; King Ahaz needed only to believe this prophecy and rely on Isaiah's Zion theology. The first divine address concludes in verse 9 with the admonition, "If you will not trust, then you will not endure." Verse 10 then introduces the second divine speech of the chapter, a speech that includes the giving of a divine sign to the kingdom of Judah.

How might we understand this sign from God? First, within the literary and historical context of this passage, the sign, which God initiates, serves to confirm the judgment prophecy in verses 7–9 concerning Rezin and Pekah and their countries. The sign functions as authentication of earlier prophecy. In other words, it does not serve as a prediction of a future event but as the evidence the event has already come to pass.

The Hebrew term used for this divine sign does not speak only of a miraculous act but is a word used within both miraculous and mundane contexts. For example, Exodus 4 provides an excellent example of the supernatural possibilities of this Hebrew word; the story uses the term "sign" when speaking of Moses's staff turning into a snake and his hand becoming leprous. Indeed, these signs are miraculous and to be ascribed to God insofar as they are supernatural events that do not naturally occur. Yet, Judges 6 uses the same word when Gideon asks the messenger of God to show him a "sign" that it is genuinely the messenger who is speaking to him. The sign requested by Gideon is for the messenger to stay until Gideon can enter his house and prepare food for the guest. The sign is naturalistic and commonplace: to remain and wait. In this context, it does not involve a miracle, per se. Of course, later in the Gideon story, the messenger causes the fire to come from a rock to consume the food. Strictly speaking, this supernatural action is not the sign Gideon initially requested, but it does indeed serve to heighten the original sign.

Whether a sign is marvelous or ordinary, it serves to call particular attention to God's actions. The sign confirms those actions even as it adds its own phenomenal element to the narrative. In 1 Samuel 2:34, we find a prophetic context similar to that addressed in Isaiah 7. A man of God prophesies concerning Eli, whose family was judged because of him and his wicked sons. After the prophecy of judgment occurs, a sign is given: both of Eli's sons will die on the same day. The sign and its surrounding prophecy share similarities with our Isaiah passage; the sign serves to confirm a previous prophecy. Also, the sign concerns death, a natural occurrence, but this is an unusual circumstance—the death of brothers on the same day.

Isaiah 7:13 shifts the address away from Ahaz alone to the collective House of David with the introduction of prophetic speech. The rhetorical question ("Is it a little matter . . . ?") provides further evidence of a shift to a broader audience by its use of plural verbs and objects. The sign may have begun as a matter between God and the king, but it ultimately extends to the whole kingdom of Judah. To understand this passage within its originating context, we need to note the literary addressee here. While the story certainly has power within our religious communities today, it also proved influential to the struggling and endangered kingdom of Ahaz, the House of David.

However, what exactly was the sign? Even if we know it confirmed the earlier judgment prophecy and was addressed to a plurality, it is not clear what element of the story represented the sign. Was it the young woman, her pregnancy, the name of the child, or perhaps the enemy kings' loss of land during the early years of the child's life? All seem possible candidates for the designation of a sign.

One of the most discussed aspects of Isaiah 7 concerns the young woman. She has garnered considerable attention in the history of Christian interpretation of this passage because of the focus on her virginity. In his writing, Isaiah did not have a virginal figure in mind. Her status as a virgin must be attributed to later (Christian) interpretation. Contemporary translations used in churches every week maintain the tension in countering interpretations of the passage. For example, the King James Version and the New International Version both translate the Hebrew term as "virgin," while the New Revised Standard Version and the Common English Bible both use "young woman." The Hebrew word does not focus primarily on the virginity or chastity of the woman, even though many (male) scholars and theologians through the ages have tried to direct attention there. Instead, her age and possibly her marital status are of concern: in brief, she is of marriageable age, a young woman eligible for marriage. Using this definition, she could be married, though probably without children, or unmarried. Given the sexual customs and ethics of ancient Israel, unmarried women of marriageable age were likely to be virgins, but the Hebrew word does not focus on this aspect of her life. There is, in fact, a separate Hebrew word for virgin, *betulah*. She is a young woman; virginity is not an issue.

This young woman is pregnant and about to give birth to a son. The way the verb tense is translated is important: Isaiah was likely pointing to a nearby pregnant woman, a physical condition visible to him and his audience. He used the word *Look!* to signal the woman's presence. The translation of the verb in the future tense ("will conceive") is not probable here (the Hebrew word is an adjective or participle). The exact form of the word is used elsewhere in the Old Testament referring to women already clearly pregnant. For example, in Genesis 38:24, Tamar is obviously pregnant. In 1 Samuel 4:19, the wife of Phinehas is pregnant and about to give birth. Modern translations' use of the future tense in Isaiah 7 highlights the lengths to which some translations, such as the New International Version, will go to adapt their wording to their theologies. But the text clearly says she is a young, pregnant woman (and therefore not a virgin); she will not become pregnant in the future.

The sign from Isaiah 7, at least at this point in the narrative, is not a virgin miraculously becoming pregnant at some point in the future, but a current, natural pregnancy by a young woman within Isaiah's sight. We have here in Isaiah an ancient birth announcement.[1] However, how can this birth announcement be a sign? How can this child be worthy of attention? Indeed, it seems the miracle of a virginal conception would be a better sign, but this interpretation does not consider the broader literary and historical context.

Let us pause briefly over the name of the son, Immanuel. Names of children in the Old Testament often carried significance. The ancients did not choose a name only because of the way it sounded; names delivered messages; names told stories. For example, in 1 Samuel 4:21 a woman gave birth to a boy around the time of the capture of the Ark of the Covenant (and the death of her husband and father-in-law), so she named the child, Ichabod, which means "no glory" or "where is the glory?"[2] Patricia Tull summarizes the name situation in Isaiah 7 as follows:

> When this child is named by his mother . . . she is echoing Jerusalem's confidence, showing herself to be a daughter of Jerusalem,

---

1. Patricia K. Tull, *Isaiah 1–39* (Macon, GA: Smyth & Helwys, 2010), 165.
2. Tony W. Cartledge, *1 & 2 Samuel* (Macon, GA: Smyth and Helwys, 2001), 77; see also P. Kyle McCarter, *1 Samuel*, Anchor Bible 8 (Garden City, NY: Doubleday, 1980), 115–16.

taking her stand in the midst of crisis, exhibiting a trust that will be confirmed by circumstances before her son reaches even a few years of age.[3]

God is indeed with this young woman, with the king and his kingdom, and with God's people. In fact, scholars have argued that perhaps the young woman is the wife of King Ahaz, meaning the Immanuel child would be a continuation of the Davidic line. If this were the case, the birth announcement is a sign of hope and vitality for the struggling kingdom. The kingdom will continue after the crisis because a new ruler will soon be born.

Isaiah 7 ends with a prophecy concerning the land of the two kings. The audience is guaranteed that the rulers' plans will not succeed and in a matter of a few years (when do children know to reject evil and choose good?), the crisis will be averted.

In sum, the passage describes an ordinary notion of ancient Israelite prophecy speaking to the current political situation with a theological slant. God assured Ahaz and all of Judah through the prophet Isaiah that God was with them and would help them as they faced the military attacks on Jerusalem. The word of comfort, in the form of prophecy, was accompanied by a sign, a child with a unique name—a message in and of itself—who would not be grown before the political threat had come to an end. The passage was not messianic at that point in history, although there is a plausible interpretation that works in the eighth-century BCE context. If one reads the remainder of Isaiah 7, verses 17–25, the whole context of the prophecy becomes clear.

Note how the prophecy and story of the woman and her child made sense within their historical context. As Christians, with other interpretations at our disposal, we can see how texts might change their emphases and depart from originating contexts in light of new situations and questions. We are not restrained by this eighth-century BCE context as if the original meaning of the text is the only valid interpretation. We do not live in an eighth-century BCE world of threatening Assyrian kings, but we do find in Isaiah 7 a coherent

---

3. Tull, *Isaiah 1–39*, 165.

ancient narrative with a relatively straightforward historical background that creates an understandable text within its ancient context. The passage does not demand a predictive or messianic interpretation to make sense.

The First-Century CE Context of Matthew 1

The Common English Bible translates Matthew 1:18–25 as follows:

> [18] This is how the birth of Jesus Christ took place. When Mary his mother was engaged to Joseph, before they were married, she became pregnant by the Holy Spirit. [19] Joseph her husband was a righteous man. Because he didn't want to humiliate her, he decided to call off their engagement quietly. [20] As he was thinking about this, an angel from the Lord appeared to him in a dream and said, "Joseph son of David, don't be afraid to take Mary as your wife, because the child she carries was conceived by the Holy Spirit. [21] She will give birth to a son, and you will call him Jesus, because he will save his people from their sins." [22] Now all of this took place so that what the Lord had spoken through the prophet would be fulfilled:
> [23] *Look! A virgin will become pregnant and give birth to a son, And they will call him,* Emmanuel. (*Emmanuel* means "God with us.")
> [24] When Joseph woke up, he did just as an angel from God commanded and took Mary as his wife. [25] But he didn't have sexual relations with her until she gave birth to a son. Joseph called him Jesus.

Matthew was the first to quote Isaiah 7 in relation to Jesus and frequently quotes or alludes to the Old Testament (in Greek translation most likely). He presents Mary and Jesus as the fulfillment of Isaiah 7's two figures: the pregnant virgin (as it is traditionally understood, but remember the originating context) and Immanuel. Consequently, even before the Christian season of Advent became a liturgical season in the early church, Gospel writers were making use of Isaiah to talk about the nativity. A reading of Matthew's birth narrative is served with a side of Isaiah.

The Gospel of Matthew was written to a Jewish community by a Jewish follower of Jesus, who was also a Jew. It is no surprise that this Gospel, a thoroughly Jewish piece of literature, used numerous quotations from the Hebrew Bible, the Scriptures of the Jews, to juxtapose the stories found there with the story of Jesus.[4] It would have been natural to attempt to understand the teachings and life of Jesus, a Jew, within the framework of the Hebrew Bible. Just as contemporary Christians place their life experiences in conversation with the sacred tradition including the Bible, ancient Jews also searched their Scriptures for answers to the issues of their day. The Jewish followers of Jesus would have understood their Scriptures as demonstrating that Jesus's life was in continuity with the tradition that enlivened their faith.

Matthew developed this relationship between the Bible and Jesus by using a paradigm of prophecy and fulfillment. The Gospel of Matthew uses some form of the phrase "all this took place to fulfill what had been spoken through the prophet" alongside quotations of the Old Testament.[5] Whether the Gospel writer himself or an earlier source created this paradigm is not our concern here.[6] Instead, we simply point out that this type of interpretive move is consistent with other Jewish interpretation during the period. Matthew was participating in the Jewish practice of viewing previous scriptural literature as prophecy in need of fulfillment in the present age. He did not invent the interpretive move but used it with great effect. By engaging a prophecy and fulfillment hermeneutic, Matthew offered an innovative understanding of Isaiah 7, especially as Isaiah 7 was not, to our knowledge, ever read by Jews to refer to a messiah before the writing of the Gospel of Matthew. Isaiah 7 was not seen as a prophecy in need of fulfillment within Judaism before Matthew's time.

---

4. See Matthew 1:23; 2:15; 2:18; 2:23; 4:15–16; 8:17; 12:18–21; 13:35; 21:5; 27:9–10.

5. The Gospel quotes the Hebrew Bible forty times; it uses this phrase thirteen times. See Marcus Borg and John Dominic Crossan, *The First Christmas: What the Gospels Really Teach about Jesus's Birth* (New York: HarperOne, 2007), 200.

6. See discussions in Ulrich Luz, *Matthew 1–7*, Hermeneia (Minneapolis: Fortress, 2007), 90–91 and in Borg and Crossan, *The First Christmas*, 110–17.

Other Jews had used the methodology of prophecy and fulfillment before and during Matthew's life, but no one had used it with regard to Isaiah 7 and the story of Immanuel. Matthew created an "early Christian exegetical phenomenon" in his unification of Isaiah 7 and Jesus's birth story, but this specific interpretation fit within a Jewish interpretive framework.[7] In other words, Matthew's use of Isaiah 7 represented a novel approach to that particular text but not a novel approach to reading in this manner.

To say Jesus's birth and naming fulfilled the prophet's message was to create continuity between the early Christians' biblical tradition and their new understandings of the life of Jesus. It legitimatized their understanding of his special birth and his special presence among them. As Daniel Harrington notes, "The notion of 'fulfillment' need not be taken to imply the end or evacuation of the OT tradition. For Matthew and his community, the tradition retained its significance and found its fullness in the person of Jesus."[8] Indeed, to quote from the biblical tradition demonstrated the Bible's significance for understanding the events of this Jew called Jesus. The tradition was taken seriously and reverently when used by the Gospel writers to explain current events, as can be seen at the beginning of Matthew's Gospel and the connection to biblical tradition. Raymond Brown suggests, regarding the first chapter of Matthew, "For Matthew the origin of Jesus Christ starts with Abraham begetting Isaac!"[9] Matthew was interested in drawing on tradition to create elements of continuity between Jesus and the ancient Jews. He also respected the tradition enough to draw upon it to interpret the significant events of his day. Matthew, however, did not think the tradition was somehow then unnecessary in light of Jesus, nor did he use Jesus to supplant the tradition. Matthew instead linked the significance of the tradition to the person of Jesus.

7. For the phrase, see Richard Beaton, *Isaiah's Christ in Matthew's Gospel* (Cambridge: Cambridge University Press, 2002), 91.

8. Daniel Harrington, *The Gospel of Matthew*, Sacra Pagina (Collegeville, MN: Liturgical Press, 1991), 38.

9. Raymond E. Brown, *A Coming Christ in Advent: Essays on the Gospel Narratives Preparing for the Birth of Jesus: Matthew 1 and Luke 1* (Collegeville, MN: Liturgical Press, 1988), 18.

The way that Matthew created continuity was by reading the Isaiah passage as a predictive prophecy, a prophecy that tells the long-term future. It is not clear whether Matthew thought Isaiah's prophecy had relevance to Isaiah's audience. Perhaps Matthew understood Isaiah's prophecy as working on two levels: one meaning appropriate during Isaiah's time and another meaning only revealed through Jesus's birth. Matthew did not explore this possibility or lay out his full understanding of prophecy; as noted earlier, his methodology was recognized by his audience as an ancient Jewish type of reading of Scripture. His use of the Isaiah quotation speaks to Matthew's understanding of Jesus's birth as the fulfillment of prophecy. He did not concern himself with Isaiah's originating context for the story, but was this omission because he discredited the originating context or because he had other priorities for his use of the prophecy? Either way, Matthew's shaping of the Isaiah 7 text created the potential understanding of the passage as having significance only with regard to Jesus's birth.

Matthew (or his source) was reading a version of Isaiah that was very close to the Greek Septuagint. The Septuagint translation, created around the second century BCE, some two hundred years before Matthew, rendered the Hebrew word for "young woman," *almah*, into the Greek word *parthenos*, which was an acceptable word choice; *parthenos* also can mean a woman of marriageable age but without particular reference to virginity. However, most of the time, the Septuagint translators used another word for *almah*, which meant explicitly "young woman." In fact, later Jewish translators such as Aquila and Theodotion corrected the Septuagint translation to bring it closer to the Hebrew source. The Septuagint translated *almah* as *parthenos* in Isaiah 7. While the word *parthenos* can refer to a young woman without reference to her virginity, it was used in other Greek literature to emphasize the virginity of a woman and was the regular translation in the Septuagint of the Hebrew word for virgin, *betulah*, discussed above. A direct connection concerning the concept of virginity was made back to Isaiah's original prophecy in the passage. The ancient Jewish translation affected how ancient Jews conceived of Isaiah 7 as they read the passage in translation.

Yet we know Matthew was not staying close to the Septuagint, because the Septuagint does not use the phrase "they shall name him" as Matthew does. The Septuagint reads "she will name him." The Septuagint translation follows the Hebrew in understanding the young woman as the person who would name the child. So who were "they" in Matthew's rendering of Isaiah? Ulrich Luz suggests that the readers of the Gospel of Matthew would think of themselves.[10] It is an interesting suggestion: the nascent Jewish community of Jesus followers would call him Immanuel; they would name him; and they would become part of the fulfillment of the prophecy. Ultimately, it is difficult to ascertain if this change has any interpretive value or is merely a translation mistake. Nevertheless, it moves the passage further away from its originating context and perhaps better actualizes the text for this early first-century community.

In addition, while the Hebrew text says, "a young woman is pregnant," the Septuagint translates "a virgin will conceive." We have previously discussed the rendering of the word *virgin* as well as the issue of the verb tense, so it stands to reason the Septuagint's use of the future tense might have encouraged a reader such as Matthew to see the passage as prophecy. In summary, "Specific renderings at two key points mean that the LXX [Septuagint] translation of 7:14 lends itself admirably to Matthew's interpretation."[11] In other words, if Matthew had been reading the Hebrew text (rather than the Septuagint), he may not have been able to make the connection to Jesus's birth as easily. The Hebrew text makes such a prophetic reading more difficult because of the terminology and verb tenses; the Septuagint translation opens such possibilities for predictive prophecy.

In summary, Matthew's theological move was one of beauty and reasonableness. He accomplished at least two things with his incorporation of this quotation from Isaiah 7. First, he read the text through a messianic lens to validate the virgin conception of Jesus. He demonstrated to his ancient Jewish audience that her unusual conception was not all that unusual if you were aware of the prophecies of Isaiah. Second, Matthew identified Jesus as

10. Luz, *Matthew 1–7*, 96.
11. John Nolland, *The Gospel of Matthew*, The New International Greek Testament Commentary (Grand Rapids: Eerdmans, 2005), 29.

God's presence among the people.[12] His reading of Isaiah provided his fellow Jews a plausible and helpful understanding of the prophetic passage and Jesus. The challenge for us today, frankly, is to not fixate on Matthew's interpretation of Isaiah for his Jewish contemporaries as the most helpful for us in our different context. Matthew's understanding of Isaiah 7 may be the most common reading of this Old Testament passage, but it is not the only reading available to us.

A Jewish Context: Isaiah 7:14 as Reference to King Hezekiah

Within a contemporary Jewish interpretive framework, this passage is not a part of the Jewish *haftarah* readings during the liturgical year. In other words, it is not assigned as a reading during contemporary Jewish synagogue worship. It is reasonably easy to guess the reasons for the omission. First, the passage is not as significant for Jews; it is but one of many interesting passages from the prophetic book of Isaiah. Second, the text has been read christologically by Christians for so long that it makes sense for Jews to not focus on the passage. Jews are not inclined to read in worship a passage from their Bible that has been used against them throughout the history of Jewish-Christian relations.

Yet Jews do have a history of interpreting the passage in a manner that makes sense to its historical context. Justin Martyr, the second-century Christian theologian, relayed in his *Dialogue with Trypho* that Trypho, a fictitious Jew of Justin's creation, read this passage as concerning King Hezekiah of Judah, not a messiah and certainly not Jesus. This interpretation, even if placed by a Christian on the lips of a nonexistent Jew, demonstrated nonetheless that Jews had an early, alternate interpretation, one known by some Christians. This Jewish interpretation is confirmed in the rabbinic tradition[13]

---

12. Both of these functions are argued for in more detail in Beaton, *Isaiah's Christ*, 90–97.

13. Exodus Rabbah on 12:29; Numbers Rabbah on 7:48.

and demonstrates the Jewish tradition's understanding of the plain meaning of a biblical passage.

Understanding the young child as Hezekiah, who indeed grew into a wise king of Judah, then identifies the young woman as King Ahaz's wife. Both the biblical and rabbinic tradition portray Hezekiah as a good king (an unusual depiction in a tradition that considered most of the kings evil!), so the identification of this special child with him is understandable. The ancient Israelite concept of kingship included the idea of the king as God's representative or even as God's son on earth. The name Immanuel then might be appropriately connected to the king.

Jewish interpreters generally carry forward a more historical understanding of Isaiah 7, drawn from their reading of the Hebrew text and their interest in Davidic kingship matters, while Christians generally carry forward a prophecy-fulfillment understanding of Isaiah 7, drawn mostly from a reading of the Greek Septuagint translation and their interest in Jesus as fulfillment of Scripture.

Our Contexts Today

The Isaiah 7 passage is placed within five contemporary contexts in what follows. These readings attempt to bring modern-day relevance to the passage while considering the ancient understandings we have already explored, not leaving these crucial readings in the past but pondering how they have a bearing on our present.

The Liturgical Context of the Revised Common Lectionary

Unfortunately, the lectionary begins this prophetic story midstride with verse 10, since Isaiah 7:1–9 contains the necessary information to understand the notions of a divine sign, a young woman, and the child. It is likewise unhelpful that the lectionary ends the story at verse 16, which is not the end of the passage. Difficult decisions must be made when selecting lessons for public reading in worship contexts, yet the current delineation of the lectionary reading confirms any suspicions that this passage is not meant to be read and understood on its own as an independent piece of Scripture. Instead, the passage is edited intentionally by the creators of the lectionary so that it fits with the Gospel reading for this Fourth Sunday of Advent in Year A.

In other words, the lectionary lifts selected theological concepts out of their historical and literary context in Isaiah 7 to present them in a larger, canonical role related to Matthew 1. The Gospel reading has directly affected the way the textual boundaries are drawn around Isaiah 7, resulting in an Old Testament reading that makes little sense independently. Of course, the lectionary does not intend for this passage to be read independently but always within the liturgical context of Matthew. In some ways, Matthew's reading of Isaiah has been accepted as the only appropriate one.

How do we assess the wisdom of this liturgical move and the likelihood that such an action might compromise the Scripture? In other words, are we reading enough of the Isaiah passage to get a clear sense of it or just enough to hear the famous words about a pregnant woman/virgin and her child, Immanuel? The lectionary draws our attention to the two Old Testament figures needed to make a christological move to the Gospel reading and its two figures, Mary and Jesus. For Isaiah to stand independently, as a word to us today apart from Matthew, the broader literary context of Isaiah 7 needs exploration. Of course, a sermon or teaching on Isaiah 7 does not need to focus exclusively on the historical context of Isaiah; it has relevance for today even outside its pairing with Matthew 1. However, this type of reading of Isaiah 7 will have to fight against the apparent desires of the lectionary.

For those who preach by way of this lectionary framing, I suggest the following possibility, one that remains committed to the lectionary's selections yet is open to an equal pairing that takes seriously both Old and New: we could read a slightly larger section of Isaiah 7, then preach both Isaiah 7 and Matthew 1 as true conversation partners. We could engage the historical contexts of both passages and explore the ongoing process of interpreting Scripture through Matthew's example. Then, we could move to how the Isaiah 7 passage might be helpful for us today, not as a prophecy about Jesus but as a word into our contemporary situations.

God Is with Us

Isaiah 7 affirms God is with the House of David during this challenging period of its history. The name Immanuel carries this promise to ancient Judah. As Christians, we also affirm God is with us in the person of Jesus, the Christ. Reading Isaiah 7 during Advent reminds us of this profound truth: God's promise of presence. In addition, God's presence is a theme throughout the Gospel of Matthew. The Gospel ends in Matthew 28:20 with the promise, "I will be with you until the end of the age." Thus, "the final admonition of the gospel in 28:20 and the formula quotation in 1:23 effectively bookend Matthew's gospel with the concept of the enduring presence of Emmanuel within the community."[14] Matthew reminds his first readers and readers down through the centuries of this powerful promise. So the promise of presence ties together the theological imaginations of Isaiah 7 and Matthew 1 with the Advent season. The theological promise of Immanuel (Emmanuel) may look different for King Ahaz's and Matthew's communities. Nevertheless, the promise is still available to both communities.

To speak of God's presence with us engenders the issue of God's presence with others. It is tempting to focus so much on God with us (as contemporary Christians) that we forget God was with the Israelites and their leaders and God is also with others such as contemporary Jews and Muslims. This sentiment can be especially tricky to articulate given the broader context of Isaiah 7, which proclaims that two other nations are not going to succeed in the end. Questions naturally arise. Is God still with them? Is God perhaps not in favor of their war-making? For God to be with Ahaz, does God turn away from other nations? These are enormously relevant questions for the Advent season. The season of Advent can be a time to remember and affirm God's presence to all God's creation. As Creator of the world, God's Immanuel presence does not pertain only to Christians.

---

14. Richard Beaton, "Isaiah in Matthew's Gospel," in *Isaiah in the New Testament*, ed. Steve Moyise and Maarten J. J. Menken (London: T&T Clark, 2005), 63–78, here 65.

This passage, when situated within its originating context, helps us theologically ponder such challenging issues during Advent. Whom is God with? In Isaiah 7 God promises to be with God's people, the ancient Judahites; these people are obviously not Christians. Isaiah 7 helps us to think about God's presence with others throughout history and in today's world, others who need Immanuel. How might we read this prophetic passage in ways that affirm God is present to all of God's children?

Immanuel and the Holocaust: Is God Really with Us?

In contradistinction to the previous point, the promise of God's presence is brought into question in light of the events of the Holocaust. The systematic murder of millions of people cannot relate in any simple way to God's guiding presence. How was God present at Auschwitz? Of course, there are no easy answers to the problem of radical evil. The extreme historical example of the Holocaust makes a more modest point: it is easy to read Isaiah 7 (and Matthew 1) during Advent and proclaim God is with us. It is more challenging to look at the contemporary world full of violence and racism—to name just two evils—and to proclaim the promise of Immanuel. It is easy to sing the familiar and cheerful hymns of Advent; it is often more difficult to relate those hymns of hope and promise to our current reality. Proclaimers of Advent-type hope must wrestle with such a paradox. The joyful chord of Immanuel might ring out of tune in certain situations of real trouble, so it must be a robust and complex chord that strikes our ears whatever our circumstances.

Interpreters of this passage could focus attention on the historical context of Isaiah 7, which did not involve, to be clear, a genocide, but did originate out of a real threat to the kingdom. God's promise of presence was not conjured up during a time of rest and peace; God's presence was needed during a particularly difficult time of unrest and war. Evil is nothing new; the ancients knew of violence and sin as well. The theological notion of Immanuel does not deny the reality of trauma and pain. It does not overlook the problematic realities of daily life. God-with-us is appropriately understood only in light of these tragedies. This is the message of Advent: not a watered down, feel-good idol called Immanuel but the full-bodied Immanuel of our biblical imagination.

Prophecy-Fulfillment Paradigm

As contemporary Christians, we need to rethink the prophecy-fulfillment paradigm and its disadvantages. The paradigm comes to us as a Jewish interpretive strategy used by authors like Matthew. However, it has also taken on new elements in thoroughly Christian contexts, elements that often lead to a denigration of the Old Testament and a sense of supersessionism.

We need to read anew Isaiah 7 and its relationship to Matthew 1 in light of our identity as Christians, an identity established only after the times of Isaiah and Matthew. So perhaps Matthew's promise-fulfillment paradigm is no longer helpful to us, given our changed context. We do not read Isaiah as first-century Jews in need of an explanation of Jesus's birth story but as Gentile Christians. We do not now participate in an intra-Jewish conversation about the old and the new like those early followers of Jesus did. The conversation about these texts has shifted significantly since the first century CE. Now we have two separate, established world religions with a vastly larger Christian population than a Jewish one. Now the promise-fulfillment paradigm has the potential to harm Judaism when Christians use it. The paradigm views the Jewish portion of Scripture (shared with Christians) as only full of promise, while Christianity's unique portion of Scripture is promise fulfilled. In our context, it is easy for this thinking to devolve into an understanding of Jewish Scripture as promise material awaiting significance. In other words, Christians using this paradigm begin to think of the Jewish Bible as irrelevant, incomplete, or lacking in worth.

In today's religiously pluralistic world, in our post-Holocaust Christian theologies, it is problematic for Christians to point to uniquely Christian events and connect those events to portions of Scripture we share with Jews with the phrase "in order to fulfill." We must be careful and thoughtful about our sense of "fulfillment." What do we mean by fulfillment? We use "fulfillment" to mean "to finally make sense of a previously unexplainable Old Testament passage." Yet are we open to the fact that Jews today do not see these biblical passages as being in need of fulfillment? Are we open to the possibility that these passages are not prophecies of the foretelling kind? We have more fruitful ways to think about biblical prophecy.

Translations Are Theological Statements

The Christian tradition, including figures such as Martin Luther, did not translate the Hebrew word *almah* in the best possible way in this biblical passage. Of course, the Septuagint's translation had already stretched the possibilities of this word. However, it was the Christian tradition that used a particular translation of this word to affirm their theology. This practice continues today; our Bible translations are not value-neutral. This passage and its interpretation through the centuries teach us that translations are interpretations; they are theological statements about communities. Whether a contemporary English Bible translation was translated by a committee of mainline Protestants or evangelical Protestants or Catholics will affect the translation.

Luther insisted that the Hebrew word *almah* meant "virgin" and was willing to pay one hundred guilders to the Jews if he was wrong. By the time of Luther, centuries of tradition supported the virgin interpretation, as John Sawyer notes,

> By the time Jerome sought to recover something of the *hebraica veritas* in his Latin translation, which was to win the official approval of Augustine and eventually of the whole Western Church, Christian Greek versions of many key words and phrases, like "virgin" in Isaiah 7:14, had after nearly 400 years become too widely accepted into the Church's tradition for them to be rejected in favour of an ancient Hebrew original.[15]

This realization should lead us to interpretive and translational humility. We should not hold too tightly to our translations of the Bi-

15. John F. A. Sawyer, *The Fifth Gospel: Isaiah in the History of Christianity* (Cambridge: Cambridge University Press, 1996), 44.

ble; we must be willing to rethink in light of our changing world and evolving faith. Just as we think anew in light of science and archaeological discoveries, so too should we hold our translations loosely, while holding tightly to our God.

A Bifocal Look

With our near vision, we see God's presence among us as Immanuel during Advent. With our near vision, we see the Revised Common Lectionary's reason for pairing Isaiah 7 and Matthew 1.

With our far vision, we see our need to rethink the dominant Christian promise-fulfillment paradigm. With our far vision, we see the Jewish tradition also has a compelling interpretation of this passage.

FOUR

Isaiah 9:2–7

Isaiah 9:2–7 // Nativity of the Lord–Proper I in Years A, B, C
Isaiah 9:1–4 // The Third Sunday after the Epiphany in Year A

*As long as Hanukkah is studied and remembered, Jews will
not surrender to the night. The proper response, as Hanukkah
teaches, is not to curse the darkness, but to light a candle.*

Irving Greenberg,
The Jewish Way: Living the Holidays

² The walking-in-darkness people have seen a great light;
on the ones dwelling in a land of pitch darkness, light has
shined.
³ You multiplied the nation; you made great its joy.
They were glad before you like joy at the harvest,
just as they rejoiced when they divided plunder.
⁴ For the yoke of their burden, the staff of their shoulder, the
rod of their oppressor,
you shattered as on the day of Midian.
⁵ For all the boots of those marching along, quaking, and the
garments rolled in blood
will become burning fuel for fire.
⁶ For a child has been born to us, a son given to us;
dominion was upon his shoulders;
his name was called Wonderful Counselor, Mighty God,
Father Evermore, Chief of Peace.
⁷ There will be no end to the abundance of his reign and to
peace concerning the throne of David and his kingdom,

> to prepare it and to support it with justice and righteous-
> ness from now until forever. The zeal of The Living God
> of hosts will do this.[1]

This chapter focuses first on the eighth-century BCE context of Isaiah 9 to appreciate how the original audiences would have understood the prophecy. Then it examines various early Christian contexts including the New Testament, Justin, and Jerome, noting each
interpretation of Isaiah 9. The critical influence of Handel's *Messiah*
on our Christian understanding of this passage will be addressed as
well. Finally, we explore some contemporary ways we might read
anew this prophetic passage within our own celebrations of Advent,
Christmas, and Epiphany.

The Originating Context of Isaiah 9

To know the actual historical context of this beautiful poem is difficult. We are given vivid imagery with little to no reference to events
or actual people that might help us to date the work. In fact, the
poem's great enduring strength may be its ability to transcend a particular period and speak into multiple historical situations. Poetry
often works this way. By not specifying names, the passage opens
to new possibilities with each new reading. Consequently, it is not
certain that this passage comes to us from the eighth century BCE.
Some scholars have dated it as late as after the Babylonian exile. However, its placement within the book of Isaiah amid chapters related
to the Syro-Ephraimite War provides some encouragement to read
this passage within that historical context.

We have, then, perhaps a late eighth-century context for a poem
using the motif of darkness and light. The people who have lived
in gloom and darkness now see the light and are joyful. Why? The
passage provides three reasons for a shift from darkness into light, all

---

1. The Hebrew and English versifications (division into verses) differ with
this passage. Throughout this chapter, I am using the versification of English
translations.

of which begin in verses 4, 5, and 6 with the word "for": 1) oppression has been broken; 2) battle weapons will now be destroyed with fire; 3) the birth of a child. These first two events may be linked to the military oppression either by the coalition of Aram/Syria and Israel or by the Assyrian Empire. Although the link to actual historical events is not clear, the passage is clearly expressing thanksgiving for an event of liberation. The importance of this incident of deliverance has been overlooked in theological (and even historical) discussions in favor of discussions of the child.

It is essential to pay attention to the verb tenses in our English translations. Most of the verbs in this passage should be translated using the English past tense. The passage begins by noting that the people *have seen* a great light. It continues with more past tense verbs: "you multiplied" in verse 3 and "you shattered" in verse 4. Finally, verse 6 announces the birth of a child. This is also an event that has already taken place. The child has been born. This detail of translation is essential in the originating context of this passage as we try to discern its meaning for Isaiah and his contemporaries. It is also vital because various contemporary English translations have changed the tenses in order to present the child's birth as a future event, a translation which lends itself more readily to a messianic interpretation.

The genre of this passage also helps situate the poem within a historical framework. Many scholars see in these verses a royal psalm of thanksgiving like those in Psalms 18 and 23. The poem or psalm pertains to thanksgiving insofar as the author gives thanks to God for the liberation from oppression in verses 3 and 4 (cf. Psalm 18:43). The poem pertains to royalty because the likely figure who helps or signals this liberation is the monarch (cf. Psalm 18:50). But does the celebration in Isaiah 9 concern the birth of this monarch, or could it possibly refer to the monarch's accession to the throne? At first glance, it seems evident that this passage speaks of the birth of the king. Indeed, a plain sense reading of the text emphasizes the straightforward phrase "For a child has been born to us." Yet the whole passage needs to be considered. After mentioning the child, the poem continues, "Dominion was upon his shoulders; his name was called Wonderful Counselor, Mighty God, Father Evermore, Chief of Peace." How can a child have dominion? Moreover, how can a child have such amazing titles? The poem continues, "There will be no end to the abundance of his reign and to peace concerning the throne of David and his kingdom." A child reigning on David's throne? It seems like quite a bit of responsibility.

A search for this imagery in other places of the Bible leads to Psalm 2:7, which demonstrates that child- and son-language in the ancient world could refer to the king's accession.[2] Though we might assume the language of birth and child would mean the king's birth is the reference, it is possible the birth language is linked to accessions to the throne. In summary, the passage speaks either metaphorically about a new Davidic king enthroned as such or literally about the actual birth of a new king.

However, who is this child king? The text is not forthcoming with the identity of this son, leaving scholars to conjecture about possibilities. King Hezekiah of Judah is the foremost contender.

Any discussion of the child/son leads naturally to the names or titles given at the end of verse 6. The issue is not only the meaning of these names but whether they are intended to be names related to the king's identity or merely names given to the king to honor God. In other words, is the passage trying to say something about the king or something about God through theophoric names—names that include the name or title of God to invoke God's favor—for example, as Ishmael means "God hears" or Samuel means "the name of God"?

The four names appear to straddle the line between relating to royal matters and God. Wise kings need to be wonderful counselors and peacemakers, while God is regularly depicted in the Hebrew Scriptures as a mighty warrior and a father. Later Christian interpreters will be more willing to view the names as attributes of the child/king; obviously, this type of reading affirms their overall messianic understandings of the passage. Nonetheless, if the names are read within the overall context of a celebration of royal accession, then it is most fitting to see in these titles the ideal qualities of a king who had been appointed by God to rule over God's people. Also, the titles

---

2. Egyptian parallels are also available. See J. J. M. Roberts, *First Isaiah*, Hermeneia (Minneapolis: Fortress, 2015), 150–51.

resemble the sorts of names given to Egyptian pharaohs during coronation liturgies. The king would need to be a wonderful counselor or wondrous advisor or even perhaps a "planner of wonders."[3] Scholars have worried much about the second name in the list—Mighty God—because it seems too hefty for a mere mortal. Again, we are confronted with the confounding question of whether these terms are primarily about the king or God. Does the term mean the king will be a mighty military presence, or is the name a divine one given to the king, such as Immanuel? The third title, Father Evermore or Eternal Father, images the king as a father figure to his people. The fourth title is most well-known: the king or government has a role in maintaining the well-being of the people.

In summary, Isaiah 9 fits well within its originating context. Although there are some interpretive challenges, the passage is coherent as a piece of ancient literature, an announcement of joy and the birth of a new leader. It is not necessary to portray this ruler's reign as occurring in the future, as eschatological. Likewise, it is not necessary to portray the ruler as a messianic figure. The text may seem patently messianic to contemporary Christians, but in its originating context, it functioned differently. This is not to say that Christians should abandon their traditional readings, but we should be open to multiple understandings of the text as we see how the text is interpreted differently in different historical contexts.

Early Christian Contexts

The New Testament does not quote the line "For unto us a child is born." Matthew, Luke, Paul—none of them use this now well-known verse in relation to Jesus. This fact might seem altogether odd. How can it be that the earliest Christians—really, Jews who followed Jesus—did not employ this text to speak of a messiah, especially since Matthew uses Isaiah 7, as we saw in the previous chapter, in relation

---

3. The first name here in this list suffers from the additional complexity of difficult Hebrew syntax. For a fuller discussion, see Patricia K. Tull, *Isaiah 1–39* (Macon, GA: Smyth & Helwys, 2010), 198–99.

to Jesus's birth? If he knows of Isaiah 7, then why not create the link to Isaiah 9? Why the omission?

We should note before we seek to answer this question that the Gospel of Matthew does quote a verse immediately before this passage (and arguably a part of this passage). In Matthew 4:12–16, the writer refers to Isaiah 9:1–2 and the geography used there:

> Now when Jesus heard that John had been arrested, he withdrew to Galilee. He left Nazareth and made his home in Capernaum by the sea, in the territory of Zebulun and Naphtali, so that what had been spoken through the prophet Isaiah might be fulfilled:
> "Land of Zebulun, land of Naphtali,
>   on the road by the sea, across the Jordan, Galilee of the
>   Gentiles—
> the people who sat in darkness
> have seen a great light,
> and for those who sat in the region and
> shadow of death light has dawned."
> (Matthew 4:12–16, New Revised Standard Version)

Matthew makes a connection between Jesus moving to Capernaum as he begins his ministry and Isaiah's prophecy concerning these lands. Of course, these territories in the first century were not named Zebulun and Naphtali, but Matthew connects the ancient tribal boundaries to Jesus's movement in the Galilee.

So Matthew certainly knows Isaiah 9 as a potential prophecy to quote, but he does not employ what will become the more famous line from this passage. Why? One possible explanation for the neglect of verse 6 in Matthew and the New Testament is that the Septuagint (Greek) translation does not adhere strictly to the Hebrew text and translates this young figure as an angel, a "Messenger of Great Counsel."[4] The Septuagint translates the entirety of verse 6 as follows:

4. Albert Pietersma and Benjamin G. Wright, *A New English Translation of the Septuagint: And the Other Greek Translations Traditionally Included under That Title* (New York: Oxford University Press, 2007), 832.

because a child was born for us, a son also given to us, whose sovereignty was upon his shoulders, and he is named Messenger of Great Counsel, for I will bring peace upon the rulers, peace and health to him.

Perhaps there were other reasons as well, which are now lost to history, but the early Christians, including Matthew, do not understand this passage as messianic or christological because the Septuagint created a new interpretation of the passage through its peculiar and particular translation. We have now seen in both Isaiah 7 and 9 that translation matters as a tool of interpretation. It should, therefore, come as no surprise to modern readers of the Bible that the differences among modern English Bible translations can be significant.

Justin, in the second century CE, was the first person known to use this passage from Isaiah 9 in connection with the person of Jesus. He used the Septuagint translation of Isaiah 9, including the phrase "the Angel of great counsel," to argue that Isaiah predicts Christ would be a great teacher. It is an argument about the nature of Christ, not a proof of Christ's status as messiah. Justin sought to highlight that Isaiah the prophet foreknew a certain characteristic of Jesus; Isaiah predicted Christ's role as teacher, as one who provides good advice and direction.[5]

A few centuries later, we encounter Jerome, who, in his fourth-century CE commentary on Isaiah, provided a rationale for why the Septuagint translated as it did: the translators did not want to equate a child with God. Remember: one of the names given to this child was Mighty God. Jerome, therefore, viewed the Septuagint's translation as preventing a theological quandary. Jerome's translation into Latin, the Vulgate, is more reflective of the Hebrew text than the Greek Septuagint.[6]

These three related contexts from the Christian tradition—the New Testament, Justin, and Jerome—demonstrate clearly how the text continues to develop in new contexts. When placed within the hands of new interpreters, the text means different things. Isa-

5. For more information, see Tull, *Isaiah 1–39*, 198.
6. Tull, *Isaiah 1–39*, 198.

iah 9 is loosed from its originating contexts in fascinating ways as new communities of faith actualize its possibilities. New translations of the biblical passages—the movement of an original Hebrew text into Greek and Latin—bring forth new explorations of meaning.

Handel's *Messiah*

Handel's *Messiah* has undoubtedly brought selected phrases from Isaiah 9 into our Advent celebrations.[7] Although the musical piece was not initially intended for performance during Advent and Christmas, it has become a regular feature of our season. Church and community choirs perform the stunningly beautiful and moving work each year. In fact, Handel's interpretation of Isaiah 9 may be our most influential one today. It is indeed more widely known than the text's originating context. We hear the repetitions and emphases of individual lines and phrases, and we absorb the meaning. The best way into a communal exploration of Isaiah 9 may even be to listen to Handel's rendition as a starting point for a more extensive discussion of the text, its history, and its influence. In the context of Handel's overall piece, this child's identity is apparent. He is the Messiah, Jesus. Isaiah has become a teller of the future, a common Christian understanding of the role of a prophet. Yet other contexts for this text exist, including the ones discussed here. How can a text that seems so clear when sung by a choir during Advent become richer and more complex as we investigate its originating context and its use throughout our tradition?

The libretto Handel used is based on the King James Version (and, for the psalms, the Anglican Prayer Book), which contains five names for this new ruler: Wonderful, Counsellor, the Mighty God, the everlasting Father, the Prince of Peace. We have already established the long-standing confusion about the names, including confusion about the syntax of the first name. How many? What do

---

7. For a book of reflections on the scriptural texts of Handel's *Messiah*, see Jessica Miller Kelley, *Every Valley: Advent with the Scriptures of Handel's* Messiah (Louisville: Westminster John Knox, 2014).

they mean? Are they about the child or God? Handel's libretto, set to music, answered these questions in a particular way. Handel knew of five names based on the King James Version translation. So hearers of the piece today also know of five.

How might we appreciate Handel's gorgeous interpretation of Isaiah 9 while remaining open to other readings? Asking these types of questions can help us see that Handel's familiar rendering of this passage is based on historically dependent factors such as the accepted scriptural text before him as well as his Christian context. Indeed, we are all subject to our various contexts; understanding this, we hope, will lead us to a certain sense of interpretive humility.

However, contexts sometimes collide. Our Jewish neighbors share this Isaiah passage with us as sacred Scripture; yet we will differ about whether Handel has the correct interpretation. (Of course, we may still agree that the piece is the work of a musical genius!) Our response to our Jewish neighbors will need to allow room for their non-messianic understanding of the passage. The topic of appropriate contemporary Christian responses leads to a discussion of our current context.

Our Contexts Today

Isaiah 9 is read below using four different contemporary contexts that attend to Christian liturgical practices and ethical considerations. These readings hopefully bring out various aspects of this well-known passage.

The Lectionary and Christmas Day

The Revised Common Lectionary does not prescribe Isaiah 9 as a reading during the season of Advent. This notice of the birth of a child is reserved until Christmas Day itself when it is paired with the Luke 2 story. Luke's story of the birth of Jesus combines with Isaiah 9 to create a coherent theological theme of birth. While it has the potential to affirm a prophecy-fulfillment paradigm in which the Old Testament reading is seen as merely a prophecy in need of fulfillment, alternative readings exist.

The birth of a child provides the emotional space to look back and ahead. It is the culmination of months of preparation and waiting; it is the beginning of years of caretaking and guidance. Birth stories call us to hope in the future. Christmas Day also engenders such a response. It signals the end of our waiting, our Advent dreams. The Christ child's birth brings with it a shift in our theological imaginations as waiting gives way to joy and delight. Yet the story has not concluded. We welcome this child; we welcome any child with additional anticipation of who he or she will become.

Isaiah 9 presents the opportunity to tell the story of Israel's particular longing for a king as they witnessed the birth of a young one who stood in the line of David. The Lukan narrative of Jesus's birth demonstrates that this longing persists over time. Who will this child be? How might this baby change us? These are birth questions. These are the questions of Isaiah and Luke. Strictly speaking, Isaiah's message—"unto us a child is born"—is not addressed to Christians foremost. We are not the original "us." Yet we also find ourselves in the story as we join the longing and the celebration of the birth of Jesus. The challenge presented by Isaiah 9, especially when it is paired with Luke 2, concerns Christians' tendency to regard the "us" as exclusively a self-reference.

While acknowledging that Jesus's birth carries significant theological meaning, we might also make a comparison to contemporary birth stories. The Christian tradition with its rituals of infant baptism and baby dedication understands the importance of celebrating new life or marking the hopefulness and joy that accompany a newborn.

Epiphany and Light

As noted above, Isaiah 9 is most often associated with Advent by its inclusion in Handel's *Messiah*. The association with Christmas stems from its use as a reading on Christmas Day in the Revised Common Lectionary. Isaiah 9 is also associated with the season of Epiphany as a reading on the Third Sunday after the Epiphany in Year A. The passage is read on this Sunday in conjunction with Matthew 4:12–23, which quotes Isaiah 9. As noted earlier in this chapter, Matthew quotes a portion of Isaiah 9 to demonstrate how Jesus leaving his hometown of

Nazareth to journey to Capernaum is a fulfillment of Isaiah's prophecy. The lectionary selections again provide the potential to affirm a prophecy-fulfillment paradigm in which the Isaiah reading is seen as merely a prophecy in need of fulfillment. Alternatively, we could focus on the imagery of light in both passages.

Isaiah 9:2 notes, "The walking-in-darkness people have seen a great light; on the ones dwelling in a land of pitch darkness, light has shined." As mentioned earlier, the exact historical context is difficult to ascertain, yet it remains clear that the audience for this prophecy lived in a time and space in need of illumination. Seeing this light during a time of probable military occupation brought hope concerning their future. This same sense of hope was brought to Capernaum and the region when Jesus moved there from Nazareth. This area of Galilee was under Roman occupation at the time; the people were walking in pitch darkness. Light in both passages is symbolic of deliverance and liberation from threats.

During the season of Epiphany, Isaiah 9 can help us contemplate the areas of our lives in need of illumination. We may not be living under Assyrian or Roman imperial control, but we are in search of light and deliverance. When we find ourselves in moments or seasons of despair, the world can become unnavigable. God provides a light to guide our feet and to illuminate our path.

Hanukkah, the Festival of Lights

During the Christian celebration of Advent, our Jewish neighbors celebrate Hanukkah, a Jewish festival that remembers the rededication of the Jewish temple during the Maccabean revolt in the second century BCE. Jews celebrate today by lighting candles of a menorah, saying prayers, playing with dreidels, and exchanging gelt (usually chocolate coins). The eight-day celebration is sometimes called the Festival of Lights. Perhaps it is the seasonal context of winter, but both Christians and Jews use lights during this time to celebrate. Isaiah 9 also uses this imagery to depict deliverance and liberation. Christians can learn from Jews as we together ponder how to bring people from darkness into light. As Irving Greenberg notes, "As long as Hanukkah is studied and remembered, Jews will not surrender to the night. The proper response, as Hanukkah teaches, is not to curse the darkness, but to light a candle."[8]

The Hope for a Faithful System of Government

Isaiah 9 addresses more than just a child and a great light. The passage also declares the characteristics of a faithful government over which the child has authority. When the passage has been read by Christians to affirm a prophecy-fulfillment paradigm, the focus is on verse 6; however, the passage goes on to speak of the anticipated results of this new figure's reign: endless peace, justice, and righteousness. Isaiah 9 looks forward to the establishment of these virtues in the government this new ruler brings. It is a picture of the kingdom—whether we speak of David's kingdom as it is reestablished or reformed by a historical king or of God's reign as Jesus models it. The season of Advent calls us to renewed hopes about the world concerning both concrete reforms to our systems of governance (ecclesial, municipal, state, national) and more spiritual reforms to our communal lives together.

A Bifocal Look

With our near vision, we see a wonderful child has been born to us. With our near vision, we hum along with Handel as we celebrate: "Wonderful! Counsellor! The Mighty God! The Everlasting Father! The Prince of Peace!"

With our far vision, we see our neighbors celebrating the theme of light during Hanukkah. With our far vision, we see the originating context's focus on a new king's accession to the throne.

---

8. Irving Greenberg, *The Jewish Way: Living the Holidays* (New York: Simon and Schuster, 2011), 282.

FIVE

Isaiah 11:1–10

The Second Sunday of Advent in Year A

The Rose which I am singing,
whereof Isaiah said,
is from its sweet root springing
in Mary, purest Maid;
for through our God's great love and might
the Blessed Babe she bare us
in a cold, cold winter's night.

14th century anon., trans. C. Winkworth

[1] But a branch will come forth from a stump of Jesse,
and a sprout from his roots will bear fruit.
[2] The spirit of The Living God will rest upon him—
a spirit of wisdom and understanding,
a spirit of advice and determination,
a spirit of knowledge and fear of The Living God—
[3] and his delight will be in the fear of The Living God.
He will not judge according to the appearance of his eyes;
and he will not mediate according to the rumor of his ears.
[4] But he will judge with justice the helpless poor,
and mediate with fairness the needy of the earth.
He will strike the earth with the rod of his mouth,
and with the breath of his lips, he will kill the wicked.
[5] Justice will be the waistcloth of his hips,
and faithfulness the waistcloth of his loins.
[6] A wolf will sojourn with a young ram,

and a leopard with a kid will lie down,
and a young bull, a young lion, and a fatted steer together,
and a mere youth will herd them.
⁷ A cow and a bear will graze,
together their young will lie down,
and a lion like cattle will eat straw.
⁸ A nursing child will delightfully play upon a hole of a viper,
and upon the den of a snake, a weaned child will put out his
      hand.
⁹ They will neither treat badly nor destroy on all my holy
      mountain,
for the earth will be filled with the knowledge of The Living
      God
as the waters cover the sea.
¹⁰ On that day, the standing root of Jesse
will become a flag to the peoples;
him nations will seek,
and his resting place will be honored.

This chapter begins by focusing on the originating context of Isaiah 11 in the ancient world followed by two early church readings
of the passage as examples of how the Christian tradition began to
interpret the text within Christian categories. We examine the Targum's translation of this passage in the Jewish tradition and medieval
Europe's artistic renditions of the passage in the Christian tradition.
We dialogue with a contemporary Jewish liturgical understanding
of Isaiah 11 before turning to some contemporary ways we might
read anew the prophetic passage in the light of Advent, the Revised
Common Lectionary, and the need for Christians to speak of the
Messiah without harming Jews and Judaism.

The Originating Context of Isaiah 11

The beautiful vision put forth in this passage is difficult to date
because of its lack of concrete historical references. The two major
proposals are (1) the passage is original to Isaiah, the prophet, and

refers to the Syro-Ephraimite War in which the northern kingdom of Israel was basically annexed by Assyria, and the southern kingdom of Judah was forced to pay tribute to Assyria, or (2) the passage is dated during or after the Babylonian exile, in which the kingdom of Judah and its capital city of Jerusalem were destroyed, and some Judahites were taken into captivity in Babylon. In addition to the destruction of the capital and forced migration of some people, the temple in Jerusalem was destroyed and the last king, Zedekiah, was assassinated. Dating the passage to the eighth century BCE (in other words, original to Isaiah) would make it fit well in the literary context of the preceding chapters, Isaiah 6–9. Yet the vocabulary and extreme language of "stump" fit an exilic or postexilic context as well. Both historical contexts may, in fact, be influences: an eighth-century text from Isaiah (for example, vv. 1–5) may have been expanded after the exile. Perhaps it is wise not to press too hard for a precise historical context; Isaiah 11's powerful witness to this ruler is the focus, not the historical events. The lack of historical specificity enables the passage to fit a multitude of historical settings.

The Hebrew words translated "branch" and "stump" in verse 1 are rare in biblical Hebrew. Thus, it is difficult to understand precisely what dendrological terms are referred to here. English translations provide multiple possibilities. Yet, without a comprehensive understanding of botany, we can still comprehend the imagery readily. Jesse, the father of King David, is portrayed as a stump, in other words, a cut-down section of tree, so what once stood as a mighty tree is now reduced. The line of Davidic kingship has suffered a severe blow, more than a mere pruning. Of course, a stump, with its root system intact, is not without possibilities for future growth, but it does represent a significant destructive event in the life of the tree. This passage notes that a branch, a new growth, will sprout from this stump and produce fruit again. All is not lost. Though the tree is severely compromised, it will bloom again and be productive. Read within the context of the destruction of the Davidic monarchy in 587 BCE, the passage becomes a prophecy of hope for the restoration of the monarchy by a certain figure who is characterized further. The word translated "shoot" is used in both Jeremiah and Zechariah regarding this ideal future king.[1] It is interesting to note the explicit mention of Jesse within the passage. Is this an intentional reference to David's nonpolitical and modest background? Alternatively, is it a critique of a current king such as Ahaz?[2]

Verse 2 adds more specific characteristics to this Davidic figure by noting that God's spirit will rest upon him. The phrase "spirit of The Living God" occurs primarily within the context of the judges (Othniel, Jephthah, Samson) and kings (Saul, David). Walter Brueggemann helpfully reminds us of the spirit as it comes upon David and is withdrawn from King Saul.[3] The phrase highlights the leadership and possible governing skills of such a person who is guided and strengthened by the divine spirit. This new ruler will not spring forth from devastation alone as if by his own strength. He will need the blessing and direction of the spirit to animate his reign.

Following the mention of the spirit, the prophecy lingers over three pairs of descriptors related to this spirit: wisdom and understanding, advice and determination, and knowledge and fear of The Living God. First, it is a spirit of wisdom and understanding. The word "wisdom" occurs typically in biblical books such as Proverbs, Job, and Ecclesiastes and pertains to moral conduct and character. The second pair, advice and determination, also occurs in Isaiah 36:5 (and its parallel, 2 Kings 18:20), which the New Revised Standard Version translates "strategy and power," which is also a good rendering of the lexical range of the words. This pair speaks to the need for a strategically-oriented ruler. Lastly, knowledge and fear of The Living God speaks again to a wise ruler: "the mark of a pious person, that is, the person whose socially responsible behavior is rooted in awe

---

1. Jeremiah 23:5; 33:15; Zechariah 3:8; 6:12.

2. J. J. M. Roberts, *First Isaiah*, Hermeneia (Minneapolis: Fortress, 2015), 179, notes, "The mention of Jesse, the father of David, rather than David . . . is probably to be understood as an implicit critique of the current Davidic king, presumably the disappointing and faithless Ahaz (Isa 7:9, 13), and a promise that the new David would revert to the original stock and again incorporate the ancient ideals of Davidic kingship."

3. Walter Brueggemann, *Isaiah 1–39*, Westminster Bible Companion (Louisville: Westminster John Knox, 1998), 99.

and respect for the deity."[4] Fear in this context might better be understood as reverence. This pair is brought together in Proverbs 1:7, which states, "the fear (reverence) of The Living God is the beginning of knowledge." These descriptive markers of the spirit describe the ideal leadership qualities of a king.

The next three verses (3–5) confirm this ruler's judgment and justice. The king's judgment will go deeper and not be based on mere appearance and rumor but on reality. Justice and faithfulness will be his royal attire. His attention will be given to the needy and poor in accordance with the admonition of Isaiah 1:17 to rescue the oppressed, defend the orphan, and plead for the widow. As another aspect of his justice-building, the wicked will be killed. Within the context of the ancient Near East, the administration of justice was a central feature of kingship.

Many readers notice an abrupt change in content with verses 6–10. The thematic disconnect is probably best read when we take the second half of the passage as an extension of the just kingship described in the first half of the passage. What is the result of his spirit-filled reign? His reign of justice produces a peaceful kingdom. Nevertheless, the imagery does shift from an ideal person to an ideal environment. The passage brings together animals that typically do not enjoy shared environments. Predator and prey lie together without trouble. Note how the verb "sojourn" suggests the wolf is not naturally at home with rams but must travel to a foreign land. Indeed, this type of coexistence is difficult to imagine. The youth has become a herder of these predators. The vision even goes as far as bringing a young child and a snake together. How are we to understand all these idyllic images? Perhaps it is an allegory where the animals represent various nations. The prophetic books compare foreign nations to treacherous creatures. Isaiah 5:29, for example, refers to Assyria as a lion. The prophet might have envisioned a great fellowship of nations, a time when warring countries remain at peace. An alternative interpretation sees an "allusion to a primeval time of animal peace."[5]

---

4. Roberts, *First Isaiah*, 179.
5. The phrase belongs to Joshua J. Van Ee, "Wolf and Lamb as Hyperbolic

In other words, Isaiah 11 conjures up an earlier time in which animals lived in peace to imagine the king's reign of peace.

In the end, it is a prophetic word about new, wise leadership. Within the context of either the eighth-century divided monarchy or the sixth-century exile, the passage notes the qualities of an ideal king and the epitome of good leadership. We might think of this passage in Marvin Sweeney's genre designation as an "announcement of a royal savior"[6] or even as an "accession hymn."[7] Great expectations are placed on the new ruler and his kingdom. In this passage, we have an "idealized description of a this-worldly kingdom."[8]

It is important to note that the originating context does not provide a messianic figure. Early components of a messiah concept are present in this Davidic figure and his ability to bring about a new realm. However, there are not enough elements to propose a messiah. There is no doubt that a passage such as Isaiah 11 is on the trajectory toward a notion of messianism, but it remains grounded in the reality of an earthly kingdom within the current political realm. It does not envision an end-time scenario brought about by a messianic figure.

Two Early Church Readings of Isaiah 11

The New Testament does not allude to Isaiah 11. It is not used in the Gospels to demonstrate Jesus's messiahship or his leadership as a king. This insight may be a surprise to many Christians who are accustomed to reading Isaiah 11 christologically. However, the passage is referenced by early church writers. We select two of those readings

Blessing: Reassessing Creational Connections in Isaiah 11:6–8," *Journal of Biblical Literature* 137, no. 2 (2018): 319–37; here 322.

6. Marvin Sweeney, *Isaiah 1–39*, The Forms of the Old Testament Literature (Grand Rapids: Eerdmans, 1996), 203.

7. Roberts, *First Isaiah*, 180.

8. John J. Collins, "The Eschatology of Zechariah," in *Knowing the End from the Beginning: The Prophetic, the Apocalyptic, and Their Relationships*, ed. Lester L. Grabbe and Robert D. Haak, Journal for the Study of the Pseudepigrapha Supplement Series 46 (London: T&T Clark, 2003), 74–84, here 76.

to present here as examples of how Christians found meaning in Isaiah 11 as they related this king and his reign to Christ.

The "branch" in Isaiah 11:1 was translated into the Latin Vulgate as "rod" or *virga*, which is a reasonable translation. This Latin word, however, is conveniently close to the Latin word for virgin, *virgo*, close enough for theologians such as Ambrose and Chromatius of Aquileia to make the connection.[9] Of course, they did not need the linguistic connection to make the theological connection: the Virgin Mary became the rod or the branch from the stump of Jesse. Listen to Ambrose:

> Also in Isaiah is it written: "There will come forth a rod out of the root of Jesse, and a flower will go up from his root." The root is the family of the Jews, the rod is Mary, and the flower is her Christ. When he blossoms in our land, makes fragrant the field of the soul, and flourishes in his church, we can no longer fear the cold or rain, but only anticipate the day of judgment.[10]

Ambrose provides a definite reading for these botanical images and connects Jesus to the flower emerging as life stems from destruction.

Isaiah 11:2 was regularly used by early Christian theologians to speak of the seven gifts of the Holy Spirit given to Jesus and to all who are baptized. As noted above, six attributes are associated with the spirit in the Hebrew text; the Septuagint Greek translation adds "piety" or "godliness" to the list of spiritual attributes, creating seven characteristics. Ambrose, Augustine, and Gregory the Great listed these seven gifts and cited Isaiah 11.[11] Revelation 4:5 also refers to the seven spirits of God, so Augustine read Isaiah and Revelation together. In art, these seven gifts are frequently rendered as seven doves flying around the head of Jesus. Isaiah 11 then produces a Christian

---

9. Steven A. McKinion, ed., *Isaiah 1–39*, Ancient Christian Commentary on Scripture: Old Testament 10 (Downers Grove, IL: InterVarsity, 2004), 95–96.

10. Ambrose, *Apology on David* 8.43 in *Corpus Scriptorum Ecclesiasticorum Latinorum* (Johnson Reprint Coporation, 1964) 32 2:388. Cited in McKinion, *Isaiah 1–39*, 95–96.

11. McKinion, *Isaiah 1–39*, 99–103.

understanding of the Holy Spirit as it indwells both in Jesus and in baptized Christians.

Early Jewish Translation and Interpretation of Isaiah 11

During early rabbinic Judaism, the Hebrew Bible was translated from Hebrew into Aramaic. This translation is called the Targum, which is the Aramaic word for translation.[12] The translation also introduces interpretations through its choice of certain words or its addition of a phrase; one might call it a loose translation.

The connection between verses 1–5 and 6–10 is made clear in the Aramaic translation by the addition of a profound but simple sentence at the beginning of verse 6: "In the days of the Messiah of Israel shall peace increase in the land."[13] Clearly, the translators understood this passage as messianic. Indeed, at some point between the writing of Isaiah 11 (approximately eighth–sixth century BCE) and its translation into Aramaic (approximately second century CE), the notion of a messiah had developed and was being used to read certain texts of the Hebrew Bible again. In the Christian tradition, Isaiah 11 was being read through the lens of Jesus, but in the Jewish tradition, Isaiah 11 was being read messianically. The translator perceived that only the messiah would be able to accomplish the tasks outlined in Isaiah 11 and bring about that type of kingdom. Reference to the messiah occurs in the first verse of Isaiah 11 in the Targum: "And a king shall come forth from the sons of Jesse, and the Messiah shall be exalted from the sons of his sons."[14] The metaphorical language of branch has turned concrete with the use of "king." The connection to David is also made clear with the use of "sons of Jesse" instead of "stump of Jesse." The Jewish tradition links the figure of the messiah to David just as the Christian tradition does.

12. To read the Targum in English, see The Aramaic Bible volumes published by Michael Glazier, Inc.

13. Bruce D. Chilton, *The Isaiah Targum*, The Aramaic Bible, vol. 11 (Wilmington, DE: Glazier, 1987), 28.

14. Chilton, *Isaiah Targum*, 28.

This somewhat arcane fact from Jewish antiquity reveals an important theological point. Christians—ancient and contemporary—are not the only ones to dream of a messiah. The topic is not exclusively Christian; in fact, it begins in Judaism and makes its way into earliest Christianity. Reading Isaiah 11 as if the only logical or theologically acceptable interpretation is one which concerns Jesus is historically dishonest and theologically problematic. We know other ancient readers who understood Isaiah 11 differently, that is, without reference to Jesus. Moreover, we know that ancient Jews also saw a messiah figure (who was not Jesus) in this prophetic word. Isaiah 11 with its beautiful imagery for justice and peace engenders a range of interpretive possibilities.

Tree of Jesse

During the eleventh century CE, medieval Europe provided several artistic interpretations of Isaiah 11 in the form of the Jesse tree. The most well-known is probably the Chartres Cathedral window, which dates to the middle of the twelfth century CE. At the bottom of this window, Jesse, the father of David, is depicted as sleeping. A beautiful tree emerges from his side, holding a series of kings, then the Virgin Mary, and finally Christ at the top. Prophetic figures such as Isaiah, Moses, Samuel, and Ezekiel fill out the picture, although they are not directly connected to the main tree branch growing from Jesse to Jesus. The Chartres tree is one of many Jesse trees with the depictions becoming more elaborate over time, and incorporating other figures such as the evangelists and angels.

John F. A. Sawyer argues that the popularity of the Jesse tree in medieval art is related to the cult of the Virgin Mary and medieval society's interest in royal lineage.[15] Indeed, Mary serves in this artwork as the rod (remember, in Latin *virga* is "rod" and *virgo* is "virgin") from the stump of Jesse. The art also serves another crucial theological purpose: to demonstrate Jesus's continuity with, or per-

15. John F. A. Sawyer, *The Fifth Gospel: Isaiah in the History of Christianity* (Cambridge: Cambridge University Press, 1996), 77–79.

haps better, his fulfillment of Old Testament prophecies. The tree grows naturally and inevitably from Jesse through the Davidic kings to Jesus, the Davidic Messiah of Christianity. The tree, then, does not allow for other branches to lead to other leaders. Continuity and linearity are critical in order to demonstrate the straight line from Jesse (really, David) to Jesus. It is a stylized tree with only one branch, and it may not then be able to provide contemporary Christians with the robust theological imagination we need to explore alternative ways of thinking about prophecy. The vital message of Isaiah 11 is not the accurate prophecy of direct (literal and historical) lineage down through the ages from Jesse to Jesus.

A Contemporary Jewish Liturgical Context

A local Reform rabbi in my city who regularly teaches a course on Judaism at the seminary once told our Christian seminarians: "We don't really do much with Isaiah; we leave that book to you all." Indeed, given Isaiah's canonical status outside of the Torah (the first five books of the Tanakh), Jews do not focus liturgically on Isaiah regularly. Nonetheless, passages from the Prophets section of the Jewish canon,[16] including selections from Isaiah, are used to complement the readings from the Torah. These readings are called the *haftarah* and are typically chanted. Isaiah 11:1–10 occurs as part of the *haftarah* portion for the eighth day of Passover, which concludes the festival.

The actual *haftarah* portion for that day is Isaiah 10:32–12:6. Michael Fishbane, in his commentary on the *haftarot* (plural of *haftarah*), makes two connections between the passage and the Jewish festival of Passover.[17] First, Isaiah 11:11–16 speaks of a new exodus that harkens back to the Exodus story which is central to the celebration of Passover. Second, the opening verses, Isaiah

16. In the Jewish Bible, the Prophets section includes Joshua, Judges, 1–2 Samuel, 1–2 Kings, Isaiah, Jeremiah, Ezekiel, and the Twelve Prophets.
17. Michael Fishbane, *The JPS Bible Commentary: Haftarot* (Philadelphia: The Jewish Publication Society, 2002), 431–38.

10:32–34, mention the downfall of an Assyrian leader, who is understood by the rabbis to be Sennacherib. The rabbis then posit that this leader's defeat occurred on the night of Passover. This event, which is told in detail in 2 Kings 19, is linked typologically to the exodus event.

We take away at least three lessons from this contemporary Jewish commentary on Isaiah 11. First, interestingly, the Jewish tradition is not particularly concerned with the in-between section in the *haftarah* reading, namely, Isaiah 11:1–10. Even though it sees the prophecy as messianic, it does not dwell on that portion of the text.

Second, the textual passage is set literarily within a broader context. The Jewish liturgical practice of reading larger portions of texts than the Christian lectionary allows for a more complete contextualization of any passage. By reading the end of Isaiah 10 and the entirety of Isaiah 11, the Jewish liturgical tradition provides a framework which more easily contextualizes Isaiah 11:1–10 historically, even if the exact period is unknown. The Christian liturgical tradition's tendency to focus on smaller textual units often robs hearers of larger contextual clues. It is imperative that these contexts are provided for people as they seek to make sense of the passage.

Third, the rabbinic tradition fills in interpretive gaps in the text. Sennacherib's defeat is interpreted—without much textual support—as occurring on the eve of Passover. As Fishbane observes,

> The defeat of Sennacherib purportedly on the night of Passover is thus testimony to the Jewish religious imagination—particularly its tendency to link acts of divine deliverance to earlier paradigms. By such associations, new historical events assume the power and often the characteristics of an ancient and foundational moment. History thus becomes a series of repetitive and confirming truths. For Jewish memory, God's redemptive acts are one such truth and the source of national hope. The festival of Passover is one ritual occasion when this truth and this hope are publicly celebrated.[18]

18. Fishbane, *Haftarot*, 438.

Christians are not the only people with religious and interpretive imaginations it seems! Fishbane helpfully explains how Judaism's notions of history and divine liberation are the lens through which it views passages.

Our Contexts Today

Isaiah 11 is now read through three contemporary contexts including the season of Advent, the Revised Common Lectionary, and the theological notion of messiah. These readings attend to both Christian ethical and liturgical concerns.

The Peace Candle of Advent

This Isaiah passage is heard on the Second Sunday of Advent when we typically light the Peace Candle. It would be appropriate then to highlight the extraordinary images of peace and wholeness in verses 6–10. The particular way peace is portrayed in this passage is somewhat unique in the Hebrew Scriptures. People are not depicted as working together in harmony; animals are described as living peacefully. Animals. Of course, the Christian tradition is rich with allegorical interpretations that view the animals as people or nations.[19] John Calvin notes,

> Though Isaiah says that the wild and the tame beasts will live in harmony, that the blessing of God may be clearly and fully manifested, yet he chiefly means what I have said, that the people of Christ will have no disposition to do injury, no fierceness or cruelty. They were formerly like *lions* or *leopards*, but will now be like *sheep* or *lambs*; for they will have laid aside every cruel and brutish disposition.[20]

However, humans are present in the text in that a young boy leads the animals. Either as allegory or not, the imagery is undeniably compelling

---

19. See McKinion, *Isaiah 1–39*, 105–8.
20. John Calvin, *Commentary on the Book of the Prophet Isaiah*, trans. William Pringle (Grand Rapids: Eerdmans, 1953), 1:384.

as a vision of a peaceable kingdom. Edward Hicks, a Quaker, painted several interpretations of this passage in the nineteenth century, highlighting its tranquil nature. In fact, his influence on recent interpretations of this passage is extensive.[21] Thomas Troeger has written a contemporary hymn text based on this passage entitled "Lions and Oxen Will Feed in the Hay." The hymn includes the following first stanza:

> Lions and oxen will feed in the hay,
> Leopards will join with the lambs as they play,
> Wolves will be pastured with cows in the glade—
> Blood will not darken the earth that God made.
> Little child whose bed is straw,
> Take new lodgings in my heart.
> Bring the dream Isaiah saw:
> Life redeemed from fang and claw.[22]

It would also be profitable to extend the discussion of peace back to verses 1–5 and the things that make for peace, chief among them, justice. Brueggemann is adamant about the need to place these two sections of the passage in relationship: "I suggest that the new scenario for 'nature' is made possible by the reordering of human relationships in verses 1–5. *The distortion of human relationships* is at the root of all *distortions in creation*."[23] The peaceable kingdom is possible only with the implementation of justice by a spirit-filled ruler. Thus, the passage provides Advent hope for a better, more peaceful world while also describing one way to accomplish such a vision.

Revised Common Lectionary: John the Baptist and Matthew 3:1–12

As noted above, Isaiah 11 is not alluded to in the New Testament. However, there is a similar dendrological image used by John the

21. John F. A. Sawyer, *Isaiah through the Centuries,* Wiley Blackwell Bible Commentaries (Hoboken, NJ: Wiley Blackwell, 2018), 87.

22. Thomas H. Troeger, "Lions and Oxen Will Feed in the Hay," in *New Hymns for the Life of the Church: To Make Our Prayer and Music One* (Oxford: Oxford University Press, 1992), 58.

23. Brueggemann, *Isaiah 1–39,* 102; italics original.

Baptist in Matthew 3. Thus, the Revised Common Lectionary puts these two readings together during Advent. Despite this pairing, Matthew 3 quotes from a different section of Isaiah (40:3). Isaiah 40 is read as an Advent text in chapter 9, and it would be profitable to read Isaiah 40 instead of Isaiah 11 alongside Matthew 3.

In Matthew 3, John preached repentance, and the religious leaders responded to his call. However, John called them a "brood of vipers" and commanded them to bear fruit, proclaiming, "Even now the ax is lying at the root of the trees; every tree therefore that does not bear good fruit is cut down and thrown into the fire" (verse 10, New Revised Standard Version). The imagery is somewhat similar to that of Isaiah 11, yet important distinctions are necessary. John called his fellow Jews not to rely solely on religious heritage ("We have Abraham as our ancestor") but to live faithful lives. The ax and fire then became symbols of the threat of punishment for those "trees" who do not bear fruit. Fruitless trees were otiose in John's eyes. When interpreting Matthew 3 today, Christians must be careful not to portray first-century Jews as evil people in need of repentance. John's label for the Pharisees and Sadducees does not consider their sincerity of faith; the Gospel of Matthew uses these Jewish leaders as opponents of Jesus's ministry, opposition that is already foreshadowed in their interactions with John. In contrast to Matthew 3, in Isaiah 11, Jesse's tree has already become a stump; judgment has fallen already, so the oracle sings a more hopeful tune about the possibility of new growth.

Claiming Jesus as Messiah without Harming Jews

The Christian tradition finds in Isaiah 11 the characteristics of a messiah and his kingdom of justice and peace and naturally attaches these qualities to Jesus. That is different than saying that Isaiah, the prophet, prophesied about Jesus. The first statement makes sense theologically and historically out of an ancient prophecy that yearns for an ideal ruler in light of the experience of early Christians who felt they had found this ideal person and were experiencing some of these incredible features of his kingdom. The statement leaves open the possibility that the text could be applied to other periods and other rulers. It provides a general and inspirational portrait of leadership that could be applied to several rulers. The second statement seems dangerously close to limiting the prophet's future-telling to only a Christian future. It draws a straight line between Isaiah and Jesus in a way that implies Jesus is the only possible referent for this text. Christians can embrace Isaiah 11 and its beautiful imagery of justice and peace as a part of the vision that Jesus as the Messiah brings through his life, death, and resurrection without the need for the notion of prophecy as prediction.

A Bifocal Look

With our near vision, we see a beautiful image of the peaceable kingdom for our Advent longings.

With our far vision, we claim Jesus as the Messiah with humility and the knowledge that our Jewish friends also value peace.

SIX

Isaiah 61:1–4, 8–11

Third Sunday of Advent in Year B

Come, build a land where the mantles of praises
Resound from spirits once faint and once weak;
Where like oaks of righteousness stand her people.
Oh, come build the land, my people we seek.[1]

[1] The spirit of The Living God is upon me,
because The Living God anointed me.
God has sent me out
to bear tidings of good news to the poor,
to piece back together the heartbroken,
to proclaim to captives—liberty,
and to those bound up—an opening up,
[2] to proclaim a year of pleasure belonging to The Living God
and a day of vengeance belonging to our God,
to comfort all mourners,
[3] to provide for the mourners of Zion,
to give to them a head covering instead of ashes,
oil of rejoicing instead of mourning,
an outer garment of praise instead of a disheartened spirit.

---

1. © 1979 Surtsey Publishing. Text by Carolyn McDade, "We'll Build a Land" in *Singing the Living Tradition*, hymn 121 (Boston: Beacon, 1993). The hymn is also titled "Creation of Peace." Hymn text adapted from an address by Barbara Zarotti at the Riverside Disarmament Conference. Thanks to my student, Linette Lowe, for drawing my attention to this hymn.

They will be called mighty trees of righteousness,
a planting of The Living God,
to show God's glory.
⁴ And they will rebuild the ancient ruins,
the former desolations, they will raise.
And they will make anew the wasted cities,
the uninhabited settlements of generation and generation.
⁸ For I, The Living God, love justice,
I hate robbery and injustice.
I will give them their rewards faithfully,
and an everlasting covenant I will cut with them.
⁹ And their descendants will be made known among the
      nations,
and their offspring among the peoples.
All who see them will recognize
that they are the descendants The Living God has blessed.
¹⁰ I will rejoice, rejoice, I say, in The Living God,
my whole being will exult in my God,
for God has clothed me with garments of salvation,
with an outer garment of righteousness, he covered me,
as the bridegroom wears a head covering
and as a bride adorns herself with her jewels.
¹¹ For as the earth brings out its sprouts,
and as a garden causes its sown things to sprout,
so The Living God will cause to sprout righteousness
and a song of praise before all the nations.

Theodoret of Cyrus, a fifth-century CE bishop, suggested, "It is not necessary that we give a detailed argumentation of the meaning of this prophecy, because the Master himself has made it clear to us."[2] The good bishop and I will need to disagree on this matter! The meaning of this astonishing prophecy calls out for discussion. This chapter provides various meanings of this prophecy. The passage originates in the nascent postexilic Judean community as an oracle

---

2. Theodoret of Cyrus, *Commentaire sur Isaïe III*, Sources chrétiennes 315 (Paris: Cerf, 1984), 264–65.

of liberation. It is then read through an eschatological and messianic lens in the Dead Sea Scrolls and the New Testament, a reading that continues into Jewish and Christian interpretive traditions. Today we as Christians continue to hear the essence of the ministry of Jesus in these words even as we await his coming during Advent.

The Originating Context of Isaiah 61

Isaiah 61, as an important part of Third Isaiah (Isaiah 56–66), echoes the vocabulary and theology of Second Isaiah (Isaiah 40–55) and continues the Isaian prophetic tradition into the postexilic era. While Isaiah, the eighth-century BCE prophet, did not contribute directly to the literature in the second half of the book named after him, the material certainly stands in continuity with his message. Although there are problems with such generalizations, the book of Isaiah is divided in contemporary biblical scholarship into three sections:

First Isaiah	Isaiah 1–39	preexilic context
Second Isaiah	Isaiah 40–55	exilic context
Third Isaiah	Isaiah 56–66	postexilic context

These divisions are based on vocabulary, tone, theology, and historical markers in the text. Isaiah 61 did not originate with the prophet Isaiah himself. Rather, this chapter originated in the fertile soil of the postexilic Judean community living under the rule of the newly empowered Persian Empire. It was a community in need of hope as they attempted to rebuild the temple and leadership after the devastating effects of the Babylonian exile.

If Isaiah is not the historical speaker of this oracle, who is speaking? A prophet? A kingly figure? A priest? All three possibilities have been proposed and defended.[3] Given the passage's reliance on Isaiah 42, some scholars have posited that the speaker is the servant

---

3. For a summary of recent biblical scholarship on this passage, see Randall Heskett, *Messianism within the Scriptural Scrolls of Isaiah*, The Library of Hebrew Bible/Old Testament Studies 456 (New York: T&T Clark, 2007), 225–44.

figure of Second Isaiah or his disciple. In Isaiah 42, the servant is announced as one who has God's spirit, as one who will open the eyes of the blind and free prisoners. In our passage, the spirit of God is upon the speaker, a prophetic motif. Additionally, the speaker's actions could be considered prophetic (and certainly were in later interpretive traditions discussed below). God also anoints him. Kings and priests are typically anointed in the Hebrew Bible. The verbal root for "anoint" provides the later concept of messiah, the anointed one. Perhaps the speaker is the prophet/author of Third Isaiah, and we are to read this chapter as a call story, although it is admittedly different from the call stories found in Isaiah 6 and Jeremiah 1. In this reading, the prophet—not Isaiah but a postexilic leader—received a commission from God concerning his responsibilities to liberation. Marvin Sweeney reads the anointed figure as a priest, Joshua ben Je-hozadak, the first high priest for the Second Temple. He argues that prophets were not anointed in ancient Israel; priests and kings were.[4] No matter the speaker's identity, the text is clear that the figure has received God's anointing spirit. His actions are of more importance than his identity. In fact, the passage is not as concerned about the identity of this voice as are later commentators. It may not be fruitful to try to discern too concretely the ancient figure's identity as long as we keep in mind his role as a leader in postexilic Judah.

The first four verses of this passage are divided into two sections: the first section deals directly with the figure's anointing and pro-phetic tasks (verses 1–3a); the second section speaks about the ef-fects for the people who are privy to this anointed leadership (verses 3b–4).[5] In the first section, it is hard not to recall King David, given the dual motifs of anointing and spirit.[6] 1 Samuel 16:13a states, "Sam-uel took the horn of oil and anointed him [David] in the midst of his brothers. And the spirit of The Living God entered David from that day going forward." The figure is anointed to proclaim good news, re-

4. Marvin Sweeney, *Isaiah 40–66*, The Forms of the Old Testament Litera-ture 19 (Grand Rapids: Eerdmans, 2016), 332.

5. We are following loosely Sweeney, *Isaiah 40–66*, 312–13, 318.

6. Walter Brueggemann, *Isaiah 40–66*, Westminster Bible Companion (Louisville: Westminster John Knox, 1998), 212.

lease, and jubilee. These are words of hope and comfort addressed to the poor, the heartbroken, captives, prisoners, and mourners. While it may be that spiritual destitution is in mind as well, the common meaning of these words points in a socioeconomic direction. They fit the beleaguered context of the postexilic community well. With the use of "good news" we are reminded of Isaiah 52:7: "How delightful upon the mountains are the feet of the one bearing good news, the one bringing peace. . . ."[7] These verses in Isaiah 61 do not appear to have an eschatological tone to them; they are not concerned with the distant future or the end of the world. The focus is on a current message of hope for the hopeless. The figure is anointed and uses the Hebrew word that will later in history be translated as "messiah," yet this period does not have a fully developed notion of a messiah.

The second section (verses 3b–4) notes the results of this restoration of the community. They will be called righteous terebinths; they will rebuild ancient ruins and renew ruined cities. The most likely historical reference here is the return of the exiles to the land of Judah and the renewal of community back in their homeland. Ruin and devastation, caused by the Babylonians' conquest of the area, are now envisioned as rehabilitated. Although the language may connote spiritual matters, the plain meaning of the text refers to physical restoration.

Verses 8–11 are best read in two sections.[8] Verses 8–9 conclude a larger subsection of text, an oracle of salvation that began in verse 7. These verses speak of God's love and hatred for specific actions. God loves justice and hates wrongdoing. These are the types of statements we associate with the Hebrew prophets. Also, God promises to make an everlasting covenant with God's people, one that will include blessings for their descendants. For a people who were threatened by destruction, the mention of descendants is a powerful assurance. For a people who rightly questioned the notion of God's covenant, given the brutality of exile, this mention of an everlasting covenant is a balm of comfort.

---

7. The root of the Hebrew word for "good news" occurs seven times in Isaiah 40–66. Prophets are not generally known for their good news.

8. Following Sweeney, *Isaiah 40–66*, 318–19.

Verses 10–11 turn to rejoicing! Sweeney labels this section a "hymn of praise."[9] Indeed, the tone of this portion is one of jubilation. While God voices verses 8–9, these final verses are spoken by the leader or perhaps the whole people, who lift praise because of God's great salvation. The speaker is like both bride and bridegroom arrayed in the splendor of God's garments; meanwhile, God is a gardener tending the shoots and bulbs. These hopeful words are a fitting ending to this chapter of promise.

Finally, the originating context of Isaiah 61 problematizes any simple modern understanding of prophecy again. If we demand that the prophet Isaiah prophesies about the distant future and the coming of Jesus, then it will be difficult to accept this passage as coming from another figure, another voice, who stands in the tradition of Isaiah but is not the prophet. Once we accept the multiple authorship of the book of Isaiah and see the book as a repository of a living prophetic tradition within Israel, we are better able to see how that tradition continued forward after Isaiah into the time of Second Temple Judaism and eventually was taken up by the early followers of Jesus.

Isaiah 61 at Qumran

Isaiah 61 takes on a clear eschatological tone in the Dead Sea Scrolls through the linkage of "a year of pleasure belonging to The Living God" in verse 2 with the final judgment day. On this day, a heavenly figure called Melchizedek will serve as the herald of liberation for captives (11QMelchizedek II 6).[10] Another scroll, 4Q521, connects the preaching of good news to the poor with the end of times (fragment 2 II 12). These connections reach beyond the originating Isaian context in order to form new associations with the end of days. The "year of pleasure" or "favor," according to Third Isaiah, does not concern

9. Sweeney, *Isaiah 40–66*, 319.
10. John J. Collins, "A Herald of Good Tidings: Isaiah 61:1–3 and Its Actualization in the Dead Sea Scrolls," in *The Quest for Context and Meaning: Studies in Biblical Intertextuality in Honor of James A. Sanders*, ed. Craig A. Evans and Shemaryahu Talmon (Leiden: Brill, 1997), 229.

the end of time. We can discern a distinction between the prophetic imagery of Isaiah 61 and the apocalyptic imagery at Qumran.

It also seems that Isaiah 61 is applied to a messiah figure, an anointed one, in this same Dead Sea Scroll text of 4Q521. There is, therefore, evidence to support a messianic reading of Isaiah 61 at Qumran before the writing of the New Testament. The two motifs of anointing and good news of release from captivity are taken from their originating postexilic context and placed into an eschatological, even apocalyptic, context of the Qumran sect. The figure takes on a more critical role for the community and becomes attached to the messianic expectations of the time. The scrolls from Qumran demonstrate how a messianic reading of certain biblical texts was beginning to take shape in the Second Temple period of Judaism. Certain expectations about this messiah figure were posited and debated among various Jewish groups.

Isaiah 61 and Matthew 11 // Luke 7

Matthew and Luke continue the eschatological interpretations of Isaiah 61 (as well as other selections from Isaiah). Matthew includes this exchange between Jesus and John's disciples:

> When John heard in prison what the Messiah was doing, he sent word by his disciples and said to him, "Are you the one who is to come, or are we to wait for another?" Jesus answered them, "Go and tell John what you hear and see: the blind receive their sight, the lame walk, the lepers are cleansed, the deaf hear, the dead are raised, and the poor have good news brought to them. And blessed is anyone who takes no offense at me." (Matthew 11:2–5, New Revised Standard Version)

John J. Collins has pointed out the striking parallels between this description of the Messiah and the discussion in 4Q521. Jesus does not answer the question directly concerning his identity as the Messiah, but he does list actions that were ascribed to the Messiah at that time. Collins describes a key difference though between the Qumran community and Matthew's community: "The Gospels differ from 4Q521 insofar as they claim that the wonderful deeds are already taking place, but they do make use of a preexisting, Jewish, messianic *Gestalt*."[11] These actions are based in part on Isaiah 61. Matthew's Jesus notes that certain portions of Isaiah 61 are occurring during his lifetime. For example, good news is shared with the poor. Isaiah 61 is no longer read in the future tense; it is in the present.

Isaiah 61 and Luke 4

Isaiah 61 appears on the lips of Jesus in Luke 4 in the story of Jesus's rejection in his hometown of Nazareth. Jesus stands up to read a scroll in the synagogue, and we hear Isaiah:

> "The Spirit of the Lord is upon me, because he has anointed me to bring good news to the poor. He has sent me to proclaim release to the captives and recovery of sight to the blind, to let the oppressed go free, to proclaim the year of the Lord's favor." (Luke 4:18–19, New Revised Standard Version)[12]

As in Matthew 11 and Luke 7, discussed above, these actions of liberation are presented as occurring in the present tense. They are not just dreaming for the future. Furthermore, the identity of the figure, which is so disputed in the originating context of postexilic Judah, is now clearly framed as Jesus. Of course, one can ponder how precisely Jesus is understood here—as prophet? as king? But the Gospel writer is clear that God's spirit and anointing is upon Jesus. He will deliver the good news! Despite a history of interpretation that spiritualizes this statement, it is evident in the context of Luke that social and economic issues are in view. These are the economically poor, not just the spiritually poor. The beginning of Jesus's ministry in Galilee is framed using the liberation concerns of Isaiah 61.

Luke 4 notes that the people who heard this declaration were at

11. Collins, "Herald of Good Tidings," 240.
12. Luke is quoting the LXX (Greek) version almost verbatim.

first amazed, but soon their marvel turned to rage: "If the people of Nazareth were shocked and offended by Jesus' sermon, what offended them was not the concept of the herald or his message, but the idea that the son of a local carpenter could claim such a role in the unfolding drama of salvation."[13] Indeed, Jesus in Luke's account does claim this role for himself. The rejection that he encounters is not the rejection of a prophetic or kingly leadership that offers good news to the poor. Their rejection is of their hometown son as this leader.

Rabbinic Interpretation

Given Isaiah 61's transformation during the time of Second Temple Judaism from a postexilic prophecy of liberation concerning an unknown figure to a messianic prophecy focusing on the end of time, it is not surprising to learn that rabbinic traditions regularly link Isaiah 61 to eschatology. For example, Elijah's mission to proclaim the eschaton and coming of the messiah is connected to Isaiah 61.

Yet, Isaiah 61, particularly the earlier verses related to the anointed figure, is absent within Jewish lectionaries. Seven "consolation readings" are prescribed for the Sabbaths following the Ninth of Ab (commemorating the temple's destruction): Isaiah 40:1–26; 49:14–51:3; 51:12–52:12; 54:1–10; 54:11–55:5; 60:1–22; 61:10–63:9. Notice how the lectionary skips over the bulk of our focal passage. We may have here another passage that became a focus within Christian interpretive traditions but not Jewish traditions.

Calvin

Calvin's interpretation of Isaiah 61 is vital in the history of the reception of this text because he argues for a both/and reading. On the one hand, he is committed to a christological interpretation of Isaiah 61 in which he affirms that Christ applies this text to himself (in Luke 4) and Christ is the speaker. On the other hand, he also

13. Collins, "Herald of Good Tidings," 240.

wishes to view the prophets (and the apostles) as witnesses to Christ and as people whom God anointed. So Isaiah can also be anointed by God to speak these words. The speaker is thus both Isaiah and Christ. However, the relationship between these two prophets is not egalitarian. Of course, Christ is "Head of the prophets" such that Isaiah's prophetic ministry contributes "in making known Christ's benefits."[14] Ultimately, Isaiah is speaking about what Christ will accomplish. Calvin is not particularly interested in Isaiah's original audience for the prophetic pronouncement.

Our Contexts Today

Isaiah 61 is read below through five contemporary contexts including the season of Advent, the Revised Common Lectionary, and the notions of liberation, covenant, and messiah. These contexts provide liturgical and ethical considerations of this biblical passage.

The Joy Candle of Advent

On the Third Sunday of Advent, many congregations light the Joy Candle in their Advent wreath. This theme can be explored profitably in Isaiah 61 in at least two ways. First, the good news proclaimed is one of joy. In fact, probably in an attempt to avoid the Christian term "good news" in its translation of Isaiah 61:1, the 2003 Jewish Publication Society Tanakh renders it thus: "He has sent me as a herald of joy to the humble." During Advent, we might ask how we are heralds of joy during this time of stress and rush. In a season of joy, it seems natural to feel otherwise. To be a herald of joy we first need to be a container of joy.

Second, verses 10–11, often overlooked in this passage, are joyful praises to God for God's incredible act of salvation and deliverance. Verse 10 begins, "I will rejoice, rejoice, I say, in The Living God, my whole being will exult in my God." The deep, abiding joy of Advent

---

14. John Calvin, *Commentary on the Book of the Prophet Isaiah*, trans. William Pringle (Grand Rapids: Eerdmans, 1958), 4:303.

is expressed in this type of rejoicing, which leads to the enumerations of God's blessings to us. God the gardener (Isaiah 61:11) wishes for our sprouting of joy.

Revised Common Lectionary: Isaiah 61 and John 1:6–8, 19–28

The Revised Common Lectionary does not pair Isaiah 61 with Matthew 11, Luke 11, or Luke 4, places within the New Testament where direct allusion occurs. Instead, the opening chapter of the Gospel of John is the selected Gospel lesson to read alongside Isaiah 61 during Advent. The verses focus on John the Baptist: we are told that John has come to testify to the light (verses 6–8), then we are given John's testimony (verses 19–28). John quotes Isaiah 40:3 in response to the Jerusalem Jewish leaders' questions about his identity. John is not the Messiah, nor Elijah, nor the prophet; John is the voice crying out in the wilderness. John is not the anointed one who will bring about the liberation depicted in Isaiah 61. Yet, he knows that this liberating announcement and work of good news are needed.

Black Theology: A Theology of Liberation

One cannot do justice to the complexity and power of a decades-old tradition such as Black theology in a paragraph or two. Nevertheless, it bears noting that Black theology emphasizes that Christian theology is a theology of liberation. James Cone proclaims, "The task of Christian theology, then, is to analyze the meaning of hope in God in such a way that the oppressed community of a given society will risk all for earthly freedom, a freedom made possible in the resurrection of Christ."[15] Isaiah 61's proclamation of good news and liberty resonates soundly with this understanding of theology. The audience in need of good news for both Isaiah and Cone is made up of the downtrodden, the oppressed, the captive. In fact, the gospel of God is precisely for these people.

One way to take this biblical passage forward into our contem-

---

15. James H. Cone, *A Black Theology of Liberation* (Philadelphia: J. B. Lippincott Company, 1970), 21.

porary lives then is to think about it in light of another Cone definition: "The task of Black Theology then is to analyze the nature of the gospel of Jesus Christ in the light of oppressed black people so they will see the gospel as inseparable from their humiliated condition, bestowing on them the necessary power to break the chains of oppression."[16] Whether we talk of the postexilic community in Jerusalem or American society in the twenty-first century, Isaiah 61 calls us to focus on the humiliated and to call for liberation, for the breaking of chains, for the proclamation of emancipation.

A Berit Olam, *an Everlasting Covenant*

A number of covenants exist in the Old Testament—Noah's, Abraham's (times two), Moses's, David's, Jeremiah's. Each can be viewed individually as promises from God to individuals, communities, and creation regarding specific and differing issues. For example, Noah's covenant concerns all creation, and the rainbow is a sign. Abraham's covenant involves land, descendants, and a great name with the accompanying sign being circumcision. The covenant at Mt. Sinai with Moses involves the Israelites and the giving of the Torah. Biblical scholars tend to parse out the differences among these various covenants, but theologically speaking these covenants point to a God who makes and keeps covenant with God's people. The covenant between God and God's people is constant. It may need renewing as the people tend to forget their obligations concerning the covenant, but the covenant holds. Regarding Isaiah 61, Paul Hanson notes, "At this crucial moment in history when a people, on the threshold of a new era of peace wedded to justice, flirts with the notion of serving its own self-interests, the prophet announces the steadfastness of the God who even now desires to renew the covenant."[17]

It is important for Christians to think ethically about this central biblical topic of covenant. We have a long history of supersessionist thinking in which we have often explicitly or, more recently implic-

---

16. Cone, *Black Theology of Liberation*, 23.

17. Paul D. Hanson, *Isaiah 40–66*, Interpretation (Louisville: Westminster John Knox, 1995), 226.

itly, proclaimed that the covenant that God made with Jews has been replaced by Christians (because of the Jews' rejection of Jesus and unfaithfulness to the covenant).[18] Yet, this powerful statement does not reckon with the faithfulness of God. It also suffers from a lack of understanding that Jews cannot be held responsible for the death of Jesus. It is possible for Christians to claim, as Pope John Paul II did in 1980, that Jews are "the people of the Old Covenant, never revoked by God."[19] In fact, Christians can state this theological truth more positively by noting that God's covenant with God's people, the Jews, is irrevocable. It is a gift that endures today. It is an old covenant in the sense that it is ancient in origin, but it is ever new for each generation of Jews.

When we read Isaiah 61 as Christians we must keep in mind that the everlasting covenant of God in this passage is not solely or originally for Christians. If we immediately apply the language of covenant to our Christian context without making clear that the covenant is with Jews also, then we risk the erasure of this vital faith community and world religion.

Sharing Messianic Hopes

Christians and Jews—both ancient and modern—are united in so many ways regarding their visions for a better world. These similar visions are shared partly because of our collective reliance on passages like Isaiah 61. The type of anointed and spirit-filled leadership described in Isaiah is affirmed by both faith traditions. It is essential to keep these similarities in mind even while noting the obvious differences. Christians believe the Messiah has come in the person of Jesus, while Jews do not believe this claim.

The passage from Luke 4 demonstrates that first-century Jews were not opposed to the idea of a messiah, a leader who brings good news to the oppressed. The Jews of Nazareth rejected Jesus, a fellow

18. For an excellent treatment of this issue, see Mary C. Boys, "The Enduring Covenant," in *Seeing Judaism Anew: Christianity's Sacred Obligation*, ed. Mary C. Boys (Lanham, MD: Rowman & Littlefield, 2005), 17–25.

19. Eugene J. Fisher and Leon Klenicki, eds., *Pope John Paul II: Spiritual Pilgrimage: Texts on Jews and Judaism* (New York: Crossroad, 1995), 13–16.

Jew, not because he was talking about a concept they could not understand. In fact, by quoting Isaiah 61, Jesus was participating in a typical Jewish interpretive practice.

It may be that the ideas surrounding a messiah figure in both traditions are familiar ground for shared hopes about the way the world can be.

A Bifocal Look

With our near vision, we see Jesus's liberating message to the poor. With our near vision, we see the joy of Advent as we rejoice together in God's salvation.

With our far vision, we see God's everlasting covenant with God's people, an irrevocable act of generosity and faithfulness. With our far vision, we see our shared messianic hopes about a better world.

PART THREE

Isaiah's Visions of the Future

SEVEN

Isaiah 2:1–5

First Sunday of Advent in Year A

O come, O come, Immanuel
And bless each place your people dwell.
Melt ev'ry weapon crafted for war,
Bring peace upon the earth forever more.
Rejoice, rejoice! Take heart and do not fear,
God's chosen one, Immanuel, draws near.[1]

[1] The matter that Isaiah son of Amoz envisioned concerning
    Judah and Jerusalem:
[2] In future days, the mountain of the house of The Living
    God
will be established at the head of the mountains
and will be lifted up above the hills.
All the nations will flow to it like a river.
[3] Many peoples will come and say:
"Come, let us ascend to the mountain of The Living God
to the house of the God of Jacob.
Then, God may instruct us in divine ways
that we may walk in divine paths."

---

1. Revised text by Rev. Dr. Barbara K. Lundblad, "O Come, O Come, Immanuel (Year A Verses)." Text is online at the website for the Worship Ministries of the Eastern Synod of the Evangelical Lutheran Church in Canada, http:// easternsynod.org/ministries/worship/2013/11/27/o-come-o-come-immanuel -yr-a-verses/ (accessed July 30, 2019).

For out of Zion instruction will venture forth,
the word of The Living God from Jerusalem.
⁴ The Living God will maintain justice among nations,
and mediate for many peoples.
And they will crush their swords into plowshares
and their spears into pruning knives.
A nation will not lift up a sword against a nation;
and they will not learn again war.
⁵ House of Jacob,
come, let us walk in the light of The Living God.

We begin by focusing on the originating context of Isaiah 2 in the ancient world. Then we turn our attention to this fascinating detail: Isaiah 2 is repeated almost verbatim in Micah 4. Next, we dialogue with a contemporary Jewish reading of this passage by Jewish biblical scholar Tikva Frymer-Kensky. We note how recent world political leaders have often used Isaiah's vision of peace. Finally, we read Isaiah 2 through multiple contemporary theological contexts, including the season of Advent and the Revised Common Lectionary.

The Originating Context of Isaiah 2

A straightforward title in verse 1 provides helpful literary context for this passage by labeling it as ancient Israelite prophecy. Both the Hebrew terms translated "matter" and "envisioned" are characteristic of prophetic utterances (and typically translated as "word" and "saw"). This passage is a prophecy. However, we should not automatically assume that prophecy is merely a prediction of *future* events of *judgment*. Prophecies in Isaiah (and the Hebrew Bible more generally) can be news about the past, present, or future as well as either good or bad news. To understand prophecy immediately as oriented toward the future is to read prejudicially against the common understanding in ancient Israel. Prophecy is connected with prophets. It is concerned with a divine message from God. It certainly can have future tense aspects. However, the central message of many prophets centers on the change that needs to occur now.

Because of the textual clues provided in verses 2–5, the prophecy here in Isaiah concerns the future. Furthermore, the audience for the future-oriented vision is the nation of Judah and its primary city, Jerusalem. By addressing both locales even though Judah includes Jerusalem within it, the book signals its enduring interest in the welfare of the city. While this may seem like a minor and noticeable point, it demonstrates that prophecy was typically addressed to a specific audience, an audience that is situated in history. While many peoples down through history have placed themselves as the audience of this passage, the originating audience is also evident.

The opening phrase of verse 2 indicates the time frame for the rest of the passage: "in future days" or "in the days to come" (New Jewish Publication Society), which refers to an unspecified, future period. Some interpreters have understood the time reference to concern eschatological matters, in other words, the end of time. This reading probably reads too much into the phrase since the passage speaks of a specified earthly place and does not provide other eschatological motifs. The authors of the Old Testament can write of an idealized future without referring to the end of time. We must keep in mind that the authors of Isaiah do not share the apocalyptic worldview of the New Testament writers.

Verses 2 and 3 speak of a mountain, a reference to the Jerusalem Temple Mount. Note the mountain's geographical, and therefore conceptual, superiority to the neighboring mountains. In this vivid depiction, the mountain on which the temple sits rises to become the focal object in the horizon. This imagery is consistent with representations of other ancient Near Eastern temples or worship sites that also involve high places. For example, the Canaanite deity, Baal, reigned as king atop Mt. Zaphon, north of Israel. We may also recall the Babylonian ziggurats, which serve as temples and resemble mountains (see also the Tower of Babel story in Gen. 11). The imagery in Isaiah is not meant to focus readers too specifically on a literal place but toward the specific theological traditions associated with the sacred space. Thus, the Temple Mount is to be elevated because of the presence of God and God's instruction.

The verse concludes with another image: the nations of the world streaming toward the high mountain of the temple. The Hebrew verb used here can be derived into a noun for "river," so that the nations are presented as a river flowing paradoxically up to the temple. Interestingly, the role of Israel is left unspecified. Is it merely one of the nations? Probably not. Israel's role in this vision can be assumed as central given the focus on the temple. The nations stream to the paradigmatic nation and the exemplary temple.

Verse 3 continues the imagery and theme of the previous one, using a parallel phrase, "many peoples," in place of "all the nations." The exhortation given among the peoples—they are talking to themselves—involves two poetic parallel lines:

> Let us ascend to the mountain of The Living God //
> to the house of the God of Jacob
> Then, God may instruct us in divine ways //
> that we may walk in divine paths

In the first line, the mountain and the house stand in parallel, demonstrating their essential interchangeability as labels for the Jerusalem temple. Since it is a relatively high elevation in relation to the surrounding areas, it would be natural to have to go up to the temple, but the ascension is equally symbolic. Again, we should not read the prophecy too literally with regard to space and geography. As noted above, ancient temples were often built on high ground to be closer to the heavens and easily visible from the divine realm. Jacob, the patriarch, is mentioned as part of the divine name; in fact, Jacob is mentioned almost forty times in the book of Isaiah. Perhaps Jacob's own experience of exile and return, as recorded in Genesis 25–35, serves as an exemplar for the Isaian community.

In the second set of parallel phrases, the reason for the journey up to the temple is provided: instruction in the ways of God so as to follow those ways. So, the house of God is not viewed in primarily sacrificial terms, as a place of worship, but as an institution of learning. The temple is a site of religious education that leads to ethical behavior. This understanding of temple may be perplexing to modern Christians, who principally view the Jerusalem temple in light of New Testament narratives such as Jesus's negative interaction with the place upon his entry into Jerusalem and his prediction of its destruction. However, the First Temple and Second Temple in Jerusalem functioned within ancient Judah as the center of religious life, which naturally includes sacrificial concerns as well as religious education.

The last clause of the verse switches the speaker to explain the pilgrimage in parallel lines:

> For out of Zion instruction will venture forth //
> the word of The Living God from Jerusalem

This explanation by the prophetic narrator echoes the one given by the peoples immediately before. The Hebrew word for "instruction," *torah*, is one of the richest in the Hebrew Bible, denoting much more than laws, regulations, and ordinances. The noun stems from the Hebrew verb meaning "to instruct, teach." *Torah* is a collection of religious wisdom and teachings within the Hebrew tradition. Eventually, the word will refer to the biblical books of Genesis through Deuteronomy, but at this point in the tradition, it is used more broadly to note important religious instruction.

Verse 4 shifts the focus from Zion/Jerusalem/Temple Mount to God, who is portrayed as a judge and mediator among the groups of people streaming to the temple. Although one might expect certain political, religious, cultural tensions between various national groups as they share sacred place and engage in spiritual learning, Isaiah asserts that God will manage the situation by maintaining justice. The Hebrew verb translated "mediate" is used in Isaiah 1:18 by God, in a different form, to say "let us argue it out." The verb encompasses the necessary argumentation and conversation required to reach a judgment or even reconciliation.

As a result of this harmonious situation, the people will take their now useless weaponry—swords and spears—and transform them dramatically into useful agricultural tools. Instruments of death become tools for nurturing life. The Hebrew verb used to depict this striking transformation means literally "to crush to pieces, to pulverize." Perhaps the use of such a vivid verb reflects actual understandings of the physical effort required to convert these objects into tools. Alternatively, the selection of such a powerful verb could serve a symbolic purpose to heighten the impact of the imagery. Swords do not become plowshares without considerable effort.

The final clause of the verse imagines that nations will have no reason or desire to wage war with other nations because of God's implemented justice. Divine mediation results in the loss of a curriculum for war. It is no longer necessary to fight when justice prevails. Although the implication of this verse might include the extinction also of interpersonal conflict, the focus here is clearly on the international political situation.

The phrase "learn war" also occurs in Judges 3:1–2. This passage explains that the nations, which remain after the supposedly total conquest of the land of Israel, survived so that the next generations of Israelites might be taught war. This theological justification of an incomplete conquest by the Israelites portrays the skill of war as desirable. In Isaiah 2, the skill of warfare is envisioned as obsolete and unnecessary.

Verse 5, which more naturally serves as the beginning of the next textual unit, can also serve as a bridge between the units. Jacob is mentioned again, this time as a name for the nation, Judah. Another exhortation is offered: to walk in the light of God. This coda, with its direct address to Judah, picks up the earlier pilgrimage imagery.

Intertextuality: Micah 4:1–4

Our passage from Isaiah 2 is repeated almost verbatim in Micah 4.[2] Scholars debate the direction of literary dependence: Did Isaiah take over Micah's prophecy? Alternatively, did Micah borrow from Isaiah? Or perhaps a third scenario: they both used an earlier tradition concerning Jerusalem within their writings. No matter who produced the text first, its presence in two prophetic books is remarkable and rare. The inclusion of the same text twice in the Hebrew Bible must speak to its religious relevance, popularity, and adaptability.

A close literary comparison of Isaiah 2 and Micah 4 within their re-

---

2. For a more thorough discussion of Isaiah 2 and Micah 4, see Marvin A. Sweeney, *The Twelve Prophets*, vol. 2 (Collegeville, MN: Liturgical Press, 2000), 377–81.

spective contexts highlights some particular emphases within the individual texts. For example, Micah 4:5 envisions the nations maintaining their separate religious identities even as they gather peacefully in Jerusalem ("For all the peoples will walk, each in the name of its gods"). Isaiah does not include this detail. This difference between passages provokes questions not yet asked in our discussion of Isaiah 2: Does the text envision a conversion of the nations to the Israelite religion? Is uniformity of belief the reason God can maintain justice and establish world peace? When the passage is read with these questions in mind, the vision of perfect peace is morally problematic insofar as it implies conformity on the part of the nations to the religious (and cultural and social) conventions of the Israelites. Thus, Isaiah speaks to perhaps one solution to ancient religious pluralism: conversion of all to a single religion. Micah, however, provides an alternative understanding.

Isaiah 2 and Micah 4 also relate significantly to another Old Testament passage. Amazingly, Joel 3:10 reverses the idyllic image of Isaiah and Micah and commands the soldiers to beat their plowshares into swords and pruning knives into spears as they prepare for war. They are to convert their agricultural tools for battle. In this depiction, God will sit in judgment of the nations in the valley of Jehoshaphat. While the contradiction in visions may disquiet some contemporary readers, the conflicting images allow for conversation about war and peace within the Hebrew Bible; this sacred book does not speak with a unified voice on this provocative topic. So, how do we read these opposite visions together?[3]

A Contemporary Jewish Reading

Jewish biblical scholar Tikva Frymer-Kensky has offered a recent Jewish reading of Isaiah 2:2–4.[4] She begins by noting that Isaiah 2

3. For more discussion of these passages, see James E. Brenneman, *Canons in Conflict: Negotiating Texts in True and False Prophecy* (Oxford: Oxford University Press, 1997).

4. Tikva Frymer-Kensky, "A Jewish Look at Isaiah 2:2–4," *Criterion* 41 (Autumn 2002): 20–25.

is not part of a *haftarah* reading (a selection from the Prophets, Joshua–Malachi, read weekly after the Torah selection in the synagogue). However, the phrase "For the Torah comes from Zion, the word of God from Jerusalem" from Isaiah 2 is sung as the Torah scrolls are removed from the ark each week in synagogue to be read. At the end of the reading, the congregation sings, "This is the Torah that Moses placed before Israel." Frymer-Kensky notes the beautiful tension between these two statements. The first one claims that Torah originates in Zion, a notion typical with the eighth-century prophets such as Isaiah and Amos. For them, Jerusalem is the central theological location. They do not know about—or at least they do not speak about—the Torah coming from Sinai. The second statement picks up the traditions of Exodus that Torah originated at Sinai with Moses. Frymer-Kensky says, "The bringing of Sinai and Zion together encompasses the whole history of Israel's receptivity to the once, always, and future divine instruction. Given this semiotics of Torah, it makes wonderful liturgical sense for memories of Sinai and Zion to bracket the public reading of the Torah."[5] Her comments remind Christians of the two great locales of Torah and Judaism—Sinai and Zion.[6]

Additionally, she reminds us that Zion is, in fact, a major theme of the book of Isaiah, an idea that is often unknown to or forgotten by Christians: "Their [Christians'] traditional reading of the Book of Isaiah never noticed that it is centered around Isaiah's love of Zion, which he believes will become an entirely holy city . . . , one in which no one will ever be ill or guilty."[7] When we read Isaiah through a christological lens, we neglect key theological topics such as Zion/Jerusalem because they do not contribute readily to our (Christian) understanding. It is crucial that we attend to the theological issues that are important to a biblical book in addition to the ones that are central to our identity.

---

5. Tikva Frymer-Kensky, "A Jewish Look," 22.

6. For an examination of these two concepts from a Jewish perspective, see Jon D. Levenson, *Sinai and Zion: An Entry into the Jewish Bible* (Minneapolis: Winston, 1985).

7. Tikva Frymer-Kensky, "A Jewish Look," 23.

Isaiah 2 and World Politics

Isaiah's vision of peace has often been used by political leaders who wish to speak of world political peace. For example, Richard Nixon was sworn into office as president in 1969 and 1973 with a Bible opened to Isaiah 2. In 1959, the then Soviet Union presented a large bronze sculpture, "Let Us Beat Our Swords into Ploughshares" by Evgeniy Vuchetich, to the United Nations Building in New York City. In 1967 Israel created a "Monument of Peace" in Jerusalem with the words about swords and plowshares inscribed in Hebrew and Arabic.

Our Contexts Today

I provide five different contemporary readings of Isaiah 2 below by focusing on Christian liturgical and ethical concerns.

Advent

Reading Isaiah 2:1–5 during Advent draws attention to the future orientation of the passage. As Christians look forward during Advent to the coming of Christ, Isaiah 2 looks forward to the coming of nations to Jerusalem, to instruction by God, to peace among nations. Advent and Isaiah 2 intersect insofar as they both anticipate a bright tomorrow.

This lectionary reading from Isaiah, however, was selected for the First Sunday of Advent to complement another Advent theme: the apocalypse or the end of time. Advent's intriguing tension between the first coming of Jesus as a babe and the second coming of Jesus as a culminating figure means that New Testament passages with an apocalyptic flair are read during the First Sunday of Advent. The end of the world then becomes the opening theme for Advent every year. For example, on the same Sunday as we read this passage from Isaiah 2—First Sunday of Advent, Year A—we read a portion of the eschatological discourse in Matthew 24. Furthermore, the First Sunday of Advent, Year B, assigns Mark 13:24–37, which speaks of "the

Son of Man coming in clouds," while the First Sunday of Advent, Year C, selects Luke 21:25–36, a passage also concerning the Son of Man coming in a cloud. Within this context, the Isaiah 2 passage then serves as an additional, optimistic way to envision the end of the world.

Yet, Isaiah 2 helps us think about the critical distinction between future time and end time. I contend that Isaiah 2 does not envision the end of the world. It does not belong to the set of eschatological or apocalyptic texts of the Hebrew Bible. Instead, we find in Isaiah 2 a vision for the future that is grounded in a particular place and an unspecified time. Of course, the space is idealized, and the dreams are grand—world peace and the intermingling of diverse nations—but they are dreams shared by contemporary folks today as well. Indeed, the passage claims boldly that world peace does not have to wait until the end of the world but can be established with divine assistance and judgment. Isaiah 2 helps turn our attention to the present work needed to make such a grand dream possible instead of assuming that it may take place only at the world's end.

Reading with the Revised Common Lectionary: Psalm 122

The reading of Psalm 122 for this First Sunday of Advent goes well with Isaiah 2:1–5 in that the psalm is a Zion Psalm, which concerns the glory of Jerusalem and the temple. Psalms 120 through 134 are ascent songs; in other words, songs likely used during pilgrimages to Jerusalem. Not only is the city presented as a beautiful destination ("I rejoiced when they said to me, 'To the house of The Living God we are going,'"), but Psalm 122 also speaks to the judgments that take place in Jerusalem ("For there the thrones for judgment dwell") and asks the reader/singer to pray for Jerusalem's peace ("Request the well-being of Jerusalem").

Reading with the Revised Common Lectionary: Matthew 24:36–44

It is difficult to find areas of theological and conceptual overlap between Isaiah 2 and the Gospel reading for this Sunday. Matthew 24:36–44 is concerned with the unexpected nature of the coming of the Son of Man figure. Its apocalyptic overtones would fit in with an apocalyptic reading of Isaiah 2, but, as we argue above, such a reading of Isaiah 2 is difficult. Nevertheless, a comparison and contrast between Matthew 24's end-time expectations and Isaiah 2's future time expectations prove fruitful. Both passages demonstrate the human need for meaning-making about the future even as they differ on the details and timetable.

Utopian Vision

The Isaiah 2 passage paints a utopian picture of the temple as the ideal seat of learning and a peaceful gathering place for many nations.[8] Also, the type of peace imagined, a peace in which weaponry is altogether unnecessary, participates in utopian themes. To be sure, the image of swords to plowshares conjures up notions of utopia. By utopian, we do not assert that the passage engages in unrealistic flights of fantasy, as might be connoted by the use of such a label. Utopian literature is complicated and nuanced in its depiction of places and societies. Modern literary theory concerning utopian literature highlights its significant function as a social critique of the present. While the world it envisions might not exist currently in reality and might be idealized, the literature functions to challenge the current configurations of society; the *status quo* of the present is reimagined. Some scholars argue that a utopia should not be read too literally as an exact proposal for the future; some utopian visions are not set within the future, but the present. The emphasis appears to be less on the ways things should be ideally and more on the ways things are currently wrong.

Using these theoretical insights, we might read Isaiah 2 as a critique of the current status of Jerusalem in the eyes of the world. According to the text, the city does not have the international standing

8. I have been aided in this section by some important work on biblical utopian literature. See Steven Schweitzer, *Reading Utopia in Chronicles*, The Library of Hebrew Bible/Old Testament Studies 442 (New York: T&T Clark, 2007), esp. 1–30; Ehud Ben Zvi, ed., *Utopia and Dystopia in Prophetic Literature*, Publications of the Finnish Exegetical Society 92 (Helsinki: Finnish Exegetical Society, 2006).

it rightly deserves; it is not serving as the proper center of religious and ethical learning. The city and its Temple have much to teach the nations about *torah*. God deserves a more active role in justice maintenance within the world sphere. Additionally, the passage critiques international politics and the violence afflicted between nation-states. The utopian image of swords to plowshares serves not as an impossible fantasy or even an unreachable goal. Instead, it critiques the ongoing destructive and ineffective nature of swords. The passage imagines the possibility of an agrarian society that plants and grows food as its priority.

Peace via Justice

"Justice and peace shall kiss" (Psalm 85:10b). Although the usual Hebrew words for justice (*tsedeq*) and peace (*shalom*) are not found in this passage, the concepts are alluded to and even tied together. Isaiah 2's general assessment of the interrelationship between justice and peace was echoed by Pope Paul VI in a 1972 celebration of World Day of Peace, when he asserted, "If you want peace, work for justice."[9] Verse 4 follows this same logic by noting that God will maintain justice among nations. This divine settling of arguments and mediating of competing claims is indeed a form of practical justice. The working out of justice in this manner flows immediately into the rest of the verse's depiction of sword crushing. Thus, the establishment of peace is not random or without effect; it is the result of the institution of justice.

In the twenty-first century, the phrase "world peace" is bantered about lightly too often. We have high hopes of living peacefully across religious differences, but Isaiah 2 reminds us that such dreams will not be realized fully without strong elements of justice. Although the reality of the justice envisioned by the book in this passage is problematized by its reliance on justice originating from a single religious tradition and its God while affecting diverse nations, the text nonetheless realizes that peace is a result of justice.

9. http://w2.vatican.va/content/paul-vi/en/messages/peace/documents /hf_p-vi_mes_19711208_v-world-day-for-peace.html.

A Bifocal Look

With our near vision, we long during Advent for a future full of peace and justice.

With our far vision, we see the importance of *torah* and Jerusalem within Judaism.

EIGHT

Isaiah 35:1–10

Third Sunday of Advent in Year A

Strengthen all the weary hands, steady all the trembling knees,
and say to all the faint hearts: "Courage, courage, do not be afraid.
Look, your God is coming. God comes, comes to save you.
Courage, courage, do not be afraid."[1]

[1] Wilderness and dry land will exult,
desert will rejoice and blossom like wildflower.
[2] It will sprout richly, and rejoice even with joy and singing.
The glory of Lebanon will be given to it,
the splendor of Carmel and Sharon.
They will see the glory of The Living God, the splendor of
     our God.

[3] Strengthen slack hands, and make firm unsteady knees.
[4] Say to the anxious of heart,
"Be strong, do not fear:
Here is your God! Retribution will come, the recompense of
     God.
God will come and save you."

---

1. © 1991 Martha McMane. "Strengthen All the Weary Hands," (no.
612) in *The New Century Hymnal* (Cleveland: Pilgrim, 1995). Text by
Martie McMane.

⁵ Then the eyes of the blind will be opened,
and the ears of the deaf will be unstopped.
⁶ Then the lame will leap like the deer,
and the tongue of the mute will cry out.
For waters will break forth in the wilderness,
and streams in the desert.
⁷ The dry ground will become a pool;
and a thirsty ground will become springs of water.
The dwelling of jackals will be a resting place,
an abode for reed and papyrus.

⁸ And there a highway will be,
and "the way of holiness" it will be called.
No unclean thing will traverse it,
but it will be for the one who walks the way,
and fools will not wander it.
⁹ A lion will not be there; a violent animal will not ascend
to it.
It will not be found there, but the redeemed will walk it.
¹⁰ And the ransomed of The Living God will return,
and enter Zion with shouting,
and joy forever upon their head.
Rejoicing and joy they will attain,
and grief and sorrow will flee.

This chapter first introduces the originating context of Isaiah 35. Then, we note how the Jewish tradition and Christian tradition have generally read this poem. Finally, we turn to some contemporary theological contexts for reading Isaiah 35, including the season of Advent, the Revised Common Lectionary, and the issue of suffering.

The Originating Context of Isaiah 35

This beautiful and visionary future-oriented poem lacks specific historical references, which means that it can be difficult to date. Based on themes and vocabulary, the chapter is often read as a postexilic oracle of salvation. The passage resonates with the themes of Second and Third Isaiah and was likely placed at this location in the overall book of Isaiah as a transition to that material. Isaiah 34–39 (and its subdivisions of 34–35 and 36–39) then becomes a long transitional bridge between Isaiah 1–33 and Isaiah 40–66, that is, between First Isaiah and Second and Third Isaiah. The description of the redeemed returning to Jerusalem is cast in terms of a new exodus event. The exile is over, and the people of God can return to their homeland with rejoicing.

Isaiah 35 stands in sharp contrast to Isaiah 34's depiction of Edom. Edom will move from a populated land to wilderness, while Israel will go the opposite direction. The transformation concerns nature but has clear implications for humanity as well. Read together, these chapters indicate that God's judgment on Edom leads to God's promise to Israel. It is difficult to read Isaiah 35's good news of return in isolation from God's actions against Edom. This juxtaposition creates an understandable uncomfortableness within the contemporary reader who would rather rejoice with Israel in their deliverance than denounce Edom for their wickedness. Yet, the two chapters articulate the relationship between Israel and the nations during this time. It is left to us today to ponder whether blessing for one must come only with cursing for another. Surely there is a way for all to receive deliverance.

Verses 1–2 present two disparate triads: wilderness, dry land, desert may be the current condition of the nation of Israel, but they will become like the fertile areas of Lebanon, Carmel, Sharon.[2] So the result of this environmental transformation is joy. The earth itself shall rejoice. Verses 3–4 contain the passage's commands to the people: Do not be afraid any longer, for the God of your salvation is coming. Their strength originates in God's vengeance. As J. J. M. Roberts notes, "The prophet is urging his audience to encourage one another precisely as the prophet by his message is encouraging his community."[3] Their knees need not knock against each other any longer, for they are now "Standing on the Promises."

2. Walter Brueggemann, *Isaiah 1–39,* Westminster Bible Companion (Louisville: Westminster John Knox, 1998), 275.

3. J. J. M. Roberts, *First Isaiah*, Hermeneia (Minneapolis: Fortress, 2015), 441.

Verses 5–7 continue the theme of transformation but at the human level as sight and hearing is restored. The imagery is intended to evoke a restoration of elements lost. In an ancient context in which disability was seen as something in need of healing, the image of, for example, a person who was previously unable to walk now leaping like a deer is a powerful indicator of restoration. Verses 8–10 conclude this passage by introducing the concept of a highway. Fools, unclean objects, lions, and other violent animals will not be allowed on this highway of holiness. Instead, the redeemed will walk on this highway. Redemption here is primarily physical; it is a return to Zion. It is not salvation in another world or within the heart of an individual. It is a communal event that returns the people of God to their proper place in the world—the city of God.

Rashi as Illustrative of Jewish Interpretation

Speaking generally, Isaiah 35 was interpreted in the Jewish tradition by scholars such as Rashi (eleventh-century French Jewish exegete) on a historical level as concerning the destruction of Sennacherib in Isaiah 36–37. In these chapters, the king of Assyria, Sennacherib, besieges the holy city of Jerusalem during the reign of King Hezekiah (approximately 715 BCE). He is defeated, however, after Hezekiah consults the prophet Isaiah and prays to God for deliverance. The interpretive strategy seems to be to read the vaguer non-historical poem of Isaiah 35 against the backdrop of the more historical Isaiah 36–37. Rashi views the wilderness and dry land of Isaiah 35:1 as Jerusalem/Zion, who will rejoice over the downfall of the enemies. In addition, the prophecy is read on a messianic level as concerning the age and time when Jews would be able to return to Jerusalem. The future orientation of the passage allows for this messianic interpretation. The two interpretations stand together as is common in Rashi and Ibn Ezra (twelfth-century Jewish exegete). They demonstrate the passage's ability to relate to multiple situations and the Jewish tradition's willingness to interpret at multiple levels.

Christian Tradition

Christians have generally read Isaiah 35 as prophecy in need of fulfillment by Jesus. In other words, the tradition has understood this passage as one concerning the life and ministry of Jesus, which occurs centuries after the originating context. Thus, Christian theologians provide various christological readings. Verses 5–6 are viewed in light of Jesus's ministry of healing. This connection is already established in the Gospels—Matthew 11:5 and Luke 7:22. In these passages, which will be considered further below, John the Baptist sends messengers to ask Jesus if he is the "one who is to come," in other words, the Messiah. Jesus responds by speaking of his actions in terms of Isaiah's prophecies (not just Isaiah 35:5–6, but 42:7 and 61:1). The Gospels then have Jesus model his messianic role after Isaiah's program of liberation, an interpretation that is taken up by the church fathers as well.

Our Contexts Today

Isaiah 35 is read now in five different ways that address our contemporary contexts. These contexts include Christian liturgical and ethical concerns.

The Joy Candle of Advent

Isaiah 35 is bookended with the theme of joy: the earth and nature will rejoice in the opening verses; God's redeemed people will rejoice in the closing verses. So, it is only appropriate (and joyful!) that this passage is read on the Advent Sunday in which we light the Joy Candle. This reading could even accompany the lighting ritual.

Joy is the purview of both human and humus in the future. It is not a present joy, but a joy to be anticipated; in this sense, it is an Advent joy indeed. A promise of joy. So, how do we prepare for this type of deliverance into joy? First, strengthen our weak hands and knees. Second, announce to those around us that fear is not necessary.

What would our poem of joy sound like today? How might we rewrite Isaiah 35 for our contemporary context? Anticipate joy.

Reading with the Revised Common Lectionary: Matthew 11:2–11

Matthew 11 and Isaiah 35 are brought together as Scripture lessons on this Third Sunday of Advent because of their intertextual link. Our discussion in Chapter One concerning the Revised Common Lectionary's selections during Advent noted that on the Third Sunday of Advent the Gospel readings focus on John the Baptist and his ministry. Matthew 11 begins a new section within the Gospel and focuses initially on John the Baptist, who is imprisoned. From prison, he sends his disciples to Jesus to ask him, "Are you the one who is to come, or are we to wait for another?" (Matthew 11:3, New Revised Standard Version). The question concerns Jesus's identity as the Messiah. Jesus's answer to the question points to the miracles occurring all around him. The blind see, the lame walk, the deaf hear, etc. This is the vision first shared by Isaiah—in Isaiah 35 but also throughout the book of Isaiah. These miracles of liberation are recalled again and again in Isaiah (27:19; 29:18–19; 35:5–6; 42:7; and 61:1). Jesus connects his ministry to Isaiah's vision.

There will be a temptation to read Isaiah 35 and Matthew 11 as prophecy and fulfillment. It is appealing to note that Isaiah 35 hopes for these reversals and in Matthew 11 Jesus brings them to fruition. This type of reading falters on two fronts. First, this reading depends on the problematic notion of prophecy as future-telling. It ultimately insists that Isaiah's prophecy in some fashion had in mind Jesus's future actions. Second, this reading results in an understanding of the Old Testament as an incomplete word from God. Isaiah 35 becomes an exercise in wishful thinking and dreaming that cannot possibly be realized until the work of Jesus.

Alternatively, one could speak of the hope and partial fulfillment found in both contexts. Or, even better, the dreams of a better world of joy and liberation found in both biblical passages. Isaiah 35 and its hopes of transformation are realized to an extent in the postexilic community as Jerusalem is rebuilt and the temple is reconstructed. Matthew 11 and its hopes of transformation are realized to an extent during the ministry of Jesus as he heals and preaches good news. These dreams, however, remain for us today.

Reading with the Revised Common Lectionary: Luke 1:46b–55 (Magnificat)

In addition to the Matthew 11 Gospel reading, the Revised Common Lectionary also provides an alternate "psalm" for this Third Sunday of Advent: the Magnificat from Luke 1. Indeed, the poetry is like a psalm, a song of praise more specifically. Furthermore, connections can be made between Isaiah 35's vision and the Magnificat. Even though Isaiah 35 is forward-looking and Luke 1 is responsive, both rely on great reversals—transformations—brought by God. Both provide lovely Advent longings for a better, more just world.

Disability in Verses 5–6

When discussing verses 5–6, it is easy to slip into ableist rhetoric that glorifies the non-disabled person who can see, hear, walk, and speak as one who inhabits a normative or standard body. Indeed, the ancient Israelites spoke of the normative body as "alive, whole, male, and not characterized by any abnormalities or illnesses."[4] So, it is understandable in that cultural context for the author to hope for the recovery of sight and hearing as well as the ability to walk and speak. Furthermore, the anticipated transformation can be taken as metaphorical especially since body parts are often linked to various emotions and concepts. For example, the eyes signify perception and the ears represent understanding.[5] Nevertheless, it is wise and necessary to be sensitive to the fact that these images of transformation—the blind receiving sight—carry with them certain assumptions about normative bodies.

---

4. Sandra Gravett et al., *An Introduction to the Hebrew Bible: A Thematic Approach* (Louisville: Westminster John Knox, 2008), 182.
   5. Gravett, *Introduction*, 175–76.

The Persistence of Suffering

Gene Tucker, in his commentary on this passage, has brought to our attention the "persistent human realities" that are named here.[6] The need for this type of salvation means that profound suffering exists in the background of this prophecy. He concludes: "The reader who is not willing to give up on God's concern to save will struggle to balance the announcement of God's good news with the acknowledgment that suffering persists."[7] Indeed, we need to make sure during the holy season of Advent to balance our proclamation of the good news with validation for the cries of the hurting. Advent creates a space for this type of longing for a better world and a more hopeful future. Advent marks a time liturgically to admit to ourselves and each other that deep suffering is ever present within us and among us.

A Bifocal Look

With our near vision, we see bodily transformations and healing that reminds us of our Advent hope.

With our far vision, we honor the Jewish tradition's capacity to interpret sacred texts on multiple levels.

---

6. Gene M. Tucker, "The Book of Isaiah 1–39," in *The New Interpreter's Bible*, ed. Leander E. Keck (Nashville: Abingdon, 2001), 283.

7. Tucker, "Book of Isaiah 1–39," 283.

NINE

Isaiah 40:1–11

Second Sunday of Advent in Year B

Mountains and valleys will have to be made plain;
Open new highways, new highways for our God,
Who is now coming closer, so come all and see,
And open the doorways as wide as wide can be.[1]

[1] Comfort, comfort, my people,
says your God.
[2] Speak to the heart of Jerusalem,
and call out to her
that her compulsory labor has come to an end,
that her punishment has been paid,
that she has received from the hand of The Living God
double for all her offenses.
[3] A voice calling out:
"In the wilderness clear the way of The Living God,
smooth in the desert a highway for our God.
[4] Every valley will be lifted up,
and every mountain and hill will be brought low,
and the bumpy terrain will become smooth,
and the hilly terrain a plain.

---

1. © 1972, 1993 *Centro de Pastoral Litúrgica*, admin. OCP Publications; trans. © 1989 United Methodist Publishing House, "Toda la tierra (All Earth is Waiting)" hymn. Words by Alberto Taulé. Translated by Gertrude C. Suppe.

⁵ The glory of The Living God will be revealed,
and all flesh will see it together
for the mouth of The Living God has spoken."
⁶ A voice is saying, "Call out."
And he will say, "What shall I call out?"
All flesh is grass,
and all its faithfulness is like flowers of the field.
⁷ Grass withers, flowers fade,
because the breath of The Living God blows on it.
Surely, the people are grass.
⁸ Grass withers, flowers fade,
but the word of our God will arise forever.
⁹ Ascend to a high mountain, Zion, bearer of good news.
Lift up with strength your voice, bearer of good news,
 Jerusalem,
lift it up, do not fear,
say to the cities of Judah: "Here is your God!"
¹⁰ See, The Living God is coming in might,
and God's arm rules for him.
See, God's reward is with him; God's recompense is before
 him.
¹¹ Like a shepherd, his flock he tends,
in his arms, God will gather the lambs,
and carry them in God's bosom,
and gently lead the mother sheep.

To begin the chapter, we look at the originating context of the post-exile for Isaiah 40. Then, we turn our attention to two places in the New Testament where Isaiah 40's imagery is used: John the Baptist uses this imagery in all four canonical Gospels and 1 Peter uses a different portion of the passage. Next, we see the passage's use liturgically in Jewish lectionaries as well as the portions that Calvin emphasized in his commentary. Then, we see how this passage has been shaped by its inclusion in Handel's *Messiah* and Schwartz's *Godspell*. Finally, we turn to contemporary theological issues, including the season of Advent and the Revised Common Lectionary.

The Originating Context of Isaiah 40

Isaiah 40 is marked by a long textual space as distinct from Isaiah 1–39 in both Isaiah Dead Sea scrolls from Qumran, demonstrating that even at that early stage of its transmission there was an awareness of the different quality of the material that follows in Isaiah 40–66. Scholars today would mostly agree that the book of Isaiah was not written by a single individual; instead, it is a collection of writings stemming from at least three distinct periods. As noted in a previous chapter, Isaiah, the eighth-century prophet, did not pen the second half of the book named after him. The book of Isaiah is divided by contemporary scholarship into three primary sections:

First Isaiah	Isaiah 1–39[2]	preexilic context
Second Isaiah	Isaiah 40–55	exilic context
Third Isaiah	Isaiah 56–66	postexilic context

Isaiah 40, then, begins a new section of the book of Isaiah—both in a historical sense and a literary sense. Historically, the context has shifted to the Babylonian exile, a period in which the Israelites find themselves grieving over the loss of Jerusalem, the temple, and the land. Literarily, the tone of the prophetic words shifts here in Isaiah 40 as we move from the dominant theme of judgment in the earlier chapters to the themes of promise and hope. Therefore, we situate Isaiah 40 first within an exilic context so that this originating context provides helpful background for this beautiful but succinct declaration of comfort.

One of the most basic exegetical questions—Who is speaking to whom about what?—is not easily answered in this passage. The chapter does not include a helpful superscription; instead, it begins immediately with two imperatives ("Comfort, comfort"), which are plural verbs in Hebrew. God is the commander, the speaker, here. But who is the plural addressee in this announcement? Who is the audience for this prophetic message? The Septuagint (Greek) translation clarified the situation by supplying the priests as the addressee, while the

---

2. It should be noted that some of the passages in Isaiah 1–39 are likely not original to Isaiah, the eighth-century prophet, and his preexilic context.

Targum (Aramaic) translation supplied prophets as the addressee.[3] Another option may be the angelic beings of a divine court.[4] No matter the addressee, the object in need of comfort is clear: God's people (v. 1), which is to say, Jerusalem (v. 2). It is important to note that "my people" in verse 1 is not a vocative but an object of the imperative verbs.[5] She is the one in need of assurance.

Comfort as a theological concept occurs throughout Second and Third Isaiah (49:13; 51:3, 12, 19; 52:9; 54:11; 57:6; 61:2; 66:13). It seems possible here because the people have fulfilled their service. The exile is over. Walter Brueggemann describes this type of comfort as less about solace and more about "transformative solidarity."[6] The people need reassurance after their long labor in another land.

As we move further into this passage, it is helpful to think about the overall genre of this particular passage. Many recent scholars have argued that Isaiah 40 is a scene of a heavenly court or divine council. In 1 Kings 22:19–23, Micaiah ben Imlah stands in God's court as a prophet and listens to the conversation among the "the host of heaven." This court includes divine messengers or angelic figures who serve as advisors. Isaiah 6 and Job 1 also probably have in mind these councils. If Isaiah 40 is using this image, then God is speaking—and perhaps commissioning—the prophet to speak to Israel. The court scene genre explains the conversation between God, who speaks in verses 1–2, and the other voice found in verses 3–5. Verses 6–8 then become an additional voice of another heavenly figure or the prophet's response. Also, elements of a call narrative are found in this passage, which would link this chapter to Isaiah 6, where Isaiah is called through a vision involving God in the temple. As we begin a new section of the book, and as we are introduced to an anonymous exilic prophet, it makes sense that a recommissioning takes place here.[7]

---

3. Joseph Blenkinsopp, *Isaiah 40–55*, Anchor Bible Commentary 19A (New York: Doubleday, 2002), 178.

4. Marvin A. Sweeney, *Isaiah 40–66*, The Forms of the Old Testament Literature (Grand Rapids: Eerdmans, 2016), 44.

5. See Blenkinsopp, *Isaiah 40–55*, 180.

6. Walter Brueggemann, *Isaiah 40–66*, Westminster Bible Companion (Louisville: Westminster John Knox, 1998), 16.

7. For a more thorough discussion of this passage's genre, see Sweeney, *Isaiah*

Verses 3–5 introduce a new voice—a heavenly messenger—who speaks of clearing a highway in the wilderness for God's return. The poetry's beauty matches the theological attractiveness of God's presence. Several parallel lines harken to the environmental or creational transformation that is envisioned as God returns from Babylon, from exile, to Jerusalem, to the holy city. Of course, God has taken this type of road before—the exodus from Egypt and wilderness journey was a return of God and God's people to their land.

Verses 6–8 draw a contrast between grass and blossoms, which wither up and decay, and God's word, which arises and grows forever. In other words, the image may not be as static as the usual translation of "the word of God stands forever," although standing upright is a part of the overall imagery. Meanwhile, people are impermanent like grass. The people of God are fragile and flimsy. Perhaps they are not to be trusted with the glory of God or the message of comfort from God. God's word in this context does not refer to the Bible or a text, but to the message God provides to the community.

Verses 9–11 conclude this literary unit and include commands to Zion to climb to a high mountain and lift her voice to the cities of Judah. She is the bearer of good news! So what is the good news? Brueggemann has noted that the end of verse 9 offers the key: "Here is your God!" He says, "The gospel makes the God of Israel visible and effective in a setting from which [God] had seemed to be expelled."[8] God's presence is a welcomed balm for these destitute people. The passage concludes by conjuring two divine images to elaborate on God's presence: warrior (verse 10) and shepherd (verse 11).

40–66, 46–48; Brevard Childs, *Isaiah*, Old Testament Library (Louisville: Westminster John Knox, 2000), 295–97.

8. Brueggemann, *Isaiah 40–66*, 20.

The Qumran Community and Isaiah 40

The Jewish sectarian community at Qumran applied the message of Isaiah 40 to their situation as if it were a command to them personally.[9] Scriptural interpretation was essential to their community; the Teacher of Righteousness, a leader at Qumran, interpreted Scripture within the community, and Scripture was seen as addressed to the Teacher and his disciples.[10] As residents in the wilderness, it is the community's mandate to prepare God's way in their desert setting. In other words, they shift the voice in Isaiah 40:3 to God, not a messenger figure, but they still see the way of God as in the wilderness.[11] Eugene Boring notes, "They hear themselves called to an austere life of study and discipline, as a community . . . charged to prepare the way for the coming of God, God's act of eschatological salvation effected and made real by the presence of God himself."[12] Here we see how this text of Isaiah is taken from its originating context and read in a new way to address the particular context of this Jewish community in the desert. As Scripture, it speaks to them about their needs and hopes as a sectarian Jewish movement of renewal.

The Septuagint Translation of Isaiah 40:3

In translating the Hebrew text into Greek, the translator made decisions regarding the verb "call" and the noun "voice" resulting in the

---

9. M. Eugene Boring, "From Isaiah 40:3 to Matthew 3:3—Intertextuality and Traditionsgeschichte," in *Anatomies of the Gospels and Beyond: Essays in Honor of R. Alan Culpepper*, ed. Mikeal C. Parsons, Elizabeth Struthers Malbon, and Paul N. Anderson (Leiden: Brill, 2018), 27–28, notes, "Unlike Deutero-Isaiah and his hearers, the Qumran covenanters are not transported with the prophet to the heavenly throne room, though they believe in the reality of the heavenly world in which their own worship participates in that of the angels. Yet they do not hear 'Prepare the way of the Lord' as spoken in the heavenly court to the assembled angels, but as addressed to themselves, the community of the New Covenant they believed themselves to be."

10. Boring, "Isaiah 40:3 to Matthew 3:3," 27.

11. See 1QS VIII 12–16.

12. Boring, "Isaiah 40:3 to Matthew 3:3," 28.

translation, "a voice of one calling in the wilderness." With this new translation comes new interpretive possibilities. Who is the voice? The translation does not make this clear. David Moessner argues that the Septuagint sees the "voice" in 40:3, the "preacher of good tidings" in 40:9, and the servant figure found throughout 40–55 as the same person.[13] It is difficult to ascertain with certainty the translator's intent. No matter who the voice is, this translation provides the early Christian interpretations an opening to read John as the voice in the wilderness.

Boring reminds us of the broader historical and theological point: "The truism that every translation is an interpretation applies here. The LXX was the Bible of the early church. Except for the minimal extent to which early Christian interpreters were interested in, and capable of, interpreting the Hebrew text for themselves, this means that the New Testament interpretations are interpretations of interpretations."[14] The New Testament authors were working from Greek translations and were not concerned to check the accuracy of these translations against the original Hebrew.

The First-Century CE Context of the Gospels

In all four Gospels (Matthew 3:3; Mark 1:2–3; Luke 3:4–6; John 1:23), a connection is made between John the Baptist and the voice crying out. We will discuss the Mark passage below since it is the Revised Common Lectionary selection for the Sunday on which Isaiah 40 is read. We will use Matthew and Luke here to demonstrate how Isaiah 40 is reinterpreted.[15]

In Isaiah 40 a number of voices speak so that verse 3 is translated:

---

13. David P. Moessner, *Lord of the Banquet: The Literary and Theological Significance of the Lukan Travel Narrative* (Minneapolis: Fortress, 1989), 242 n. 215.

14. Boring, "Isaiah 40:3 to Matthew 3:3," 29.

15. I am leaving aside the issue of Isaiah 40 in Q. For a treatment of that issue, see Boring, "Isaiah 40:3 to Matthew 3:3," 31–33.

A voice calling out:
"In the wilderness clear the way of The Living God,
smooth in the desert a highway for our God."

The voice, a heavenly messenger, begins his speech with two lines of parallel poetry. If we assigned letters to each of the phrases of the first line, we would have the following:

A (*In the wilderness*),
B (*clear*), and
C (*the way of The Living God*).
The second line would then be:
B (*smooth*),
A (*in the desert*), and
C (*a highway for our God*).

So, ABC, BAC—wonderfully parallel poetry. Of course, ancient Hebrew did not contain punctuation marks such as quotation marks; however, the poetic parallelism, Second Isaiah's theme of the way in the wilderness, and the Masoretic Text's accentuation all point to this reading. As we move to the Gospel of Matthew, it is important to remember that structurally "a voice" is not part of this speech, this set of parallel lines. "*A voice calling out*" introduces the speech and identifies the speaker.

In Matthew 3, John, who is himself in the wilderness, proclaims his message of repentance. Then, Matthew quotes Isaiah 40:3 about John and follows the translation of the Septuagint (probably as quoted by Mark and Q) by placing "the voice," that is, John, in the wilderness:

In those days John the Baptist appeared in the wilderness of Judea, proclaiming, "Repent, for the kingdom of heaven has come near." This is the one of whom the prophet Isaiah spoke when he said, "The voice of one crying out in the wilderness: 'Prepare the way of the Lord, make his paths straight.'" (Matthew 3:1–3, New Revised Standard Version)

Matthew uses Isaiah's "calling voice" but presents it as the voice in the wilderness; the divine messenger of Isaiah becomes the human messenger, John. And Isaiah's way of God in the wilderness becomes the way without a determined location. Matthew uses Isaiah as a prophet whose prediction is fulfilled in John. As we have discussed in a previous chapter, Matthew quotes his Bible, our Old Testament, to show how it is fulfilled. For example, Matthew 1:23 quotes Isaiah 7:14 (see Chapter 3) to present Mary and Jesus as the fulfillment of Isaiah 7's two figures: the pregnant woman and the child Immanuel. Two chapters later, Matthew uses Scripture again to link Isaiah 40 to this new prophet in the wilderness. By linking John with the fulfillment of Scripture, Matthew also links John to Jesus, who fulfills prophecy as well.[16] Boring links the theological worlds of Second Isaiah and Matthew thus: "But Matthew, too, sees the Christ event as the coming of God to be present with his people, to redeem them from their sacred, displaced exile, and to bring them home, the advent of Emmanuel, as God had promised through the prophet Isaiah."[17]

The First-Century CE Context of 1 Peter

In 1 Peter 1, the author of this letter exhorts his audience to holy living ("be holy yourselves in all your conduct," 1:15) and to love each other ("love one another deeply from the heart," 1:22). The author then grounds these appeals in the imperishable word of God as John Elliott notes, "In [verses] 24–25, scriptural substantiation for the imperishability of the regenerative word is supplied by a quotation from Isa[iah] 40:6–8, where human impermanence is compared with perishable grass and contrasted to the permanence of God's word."[18] The author of 1 Peter quotes from portions of Isaiah 40:6–8:

---

16. Ulrich Luz, *Matthew 1–7*, Hermeneia (Minneapolis: Fortress, 2007), 135.

17. Boring, "Isaiah 40:3 to Matthew 3:3," 38.

18. John Elliott, *1 Peter*, Anchor Bible 37B (New York: Doubleday, 2000), 389–90.

You have been born anew, not of perishable but of imperishable seed, through the living and enduring word of God. For "All flesh is like grass and all its glory like the flower of grass. The grass withers, and the flower falls, but the word of the Lord endures forever." That word is the good news that we announced to you. (1 Peter 1:23–25, New Revised Standard Version)

The quotation differs from the (Hebrew) Masoretic and the (Greek) Septuagint versions in fairly minor ways. The one interesting theological difference is that 1 Peter uses "Lord" instead of "God," which may be a way to read Jesus explicitly into the text as the Lord.[19]

Jewish Lectionaries

Isaiah 40 (the entire chapter) is the first of seven consolation readings from the book of Isaiah used as Sabbath reading following the Ninth of Ab, *Tisha b'Av*, a commemoration of the temple's destruction. According to Michael Fishbane, these seven readings "emphasize consolation and national renewal."[20] The readings include Isaiah 40:1–26; 49:14–51:3; 51:12–52:12; 54:1–10; 54:11–55:5; 60:1–22; 61:10–63:9. Liturgically, these seven readings are preceded by three "haftarot of admonition" which are read on the three Sabbaths leading up to *Tisha b'Av*; these readings include Jeremiah 1:1–2:3; Jeremiah 2:4–28; and Isaiah 1:1–27.[21] Therefore, every year the Jewish liturgy provides the opportunity to hear judgment and warning from Jeremiah and Isaiah in the lead-up to the remembrance of the destruction of the temple. Then, the book of Lamentations is read on *Tisha b'Av* followed by words of consolation from Isaiah on the weeks after this remembrance. The consolation readings are more than twice as numerous

---

19. See discussion in Paul J. Achtemeier, *1 Peter*, Hermeneia (Minneapolis: Fortress, 1996), 141; also M. Eugene Boring, *1 Peter*, Abingdon New Testament Commentaries (Nashville: Abingdon, 1999), 90.

20. Michael Fishbane, *The JPS Bible Commentary Haftarot* (Philadelphia: The Jewish Publication Society, 2002), 278.

21. Fishbane, *Haftarot*, 283.

as the judgment ones. Isaiah, then, serves as a voice of comfort and consolation liturgically during this period of the Jewish year.

Calvin's Reading

To demonstrate how Isaiah 40 continues to be reinterpreted through various theological and cultural lenses during its transmission through Christian history, we highlight two of Calvin's readings of select verses. John Calvin was a sixteenth-century French theologian and lawyer whose theology and biblical interpretation has had enormous influence on the Reformed tradition in Christianity.

Concerning Isaiah 40:8 and its insistence that the word of God will remain forever, Calvin notes,

> This passage comprehends the whole Gospel in few words; for it consists of an acknowledgement of our misery, poverty, and emptiness, that, being sincerely humbled, we may fly to God, by whom alone we shall be perfectly restored. . . . We are likewise taught that we ought not to seek consolation from any other source than from eternity, which ought not to be sought anywhere else than in God; since nothing that is firm or durable will be found on the earth.[22]

Here we find emphases on humanity's wretchedness and the Word of God's dependability—two themes of Reformed thought. Calvin's theology of the Word is different from Second Isaiah's, but they both contrast humanity and divinity in terms of consistency.

Concerning 40:9 and the content of the good news ("Here is your God!"), Calvin explains,

> This expression includes the sum of our happiness, which consists solely in the presence of God. It brings along with it an abundance of all blessings; and if we are destitute of it, we must be utterly

22. John Calvin, *Commentary on the Book of the Prophet Isaiah*, trans. William Pringle (Grand Rapids: Eerdmans, 1958), 3:212.

miserable and wretched; and although blessings of every kind are richly enjoyed by us, yet if we are estranged from God, everything must tend to our destruction.[23]

In Isaiah 40, the speaker, Jerusalem, relays the good news of God's appearance to the cities of Judah. God will be their deliverer. Calvin expands the audience for this good news to include Christian believers. The content of the good news in Isaiah 40 also seems to relate more to physical restoration; God is coming in might to help the exiles. Calvin speaks of blessings and happiness in the presence of God.

Handel's *Messiah*

Isaiah 40 is a favorite Scripture passage in Handel's oratorio *Messiah*.[24] The first words of the work are "Comfort ye, comfort ye my people." The opening goes on to use Isaiah 40:1–5 as its text. Thus, the tone for the work is set by the words of comfort in Isaiah 40. Later in the work, Isaiah 40:11, with its image of God as a shepherd, will be sung.

As noted in an earlier chapter, the libretto that Handel uses for *Messiah* is based on the King James Version (and, for the Psalms, the Anglican Prayer Book). The result of the reliance on this translation is the phrase, "Oh thou that tellest good tidings to Zion" as the text of Isaiah 40:9 that is used in *Messiah*.[25] This translation is probably faulty. It assumes an accusative object in Hebrew ("to Zion"). It is easier to read the Hebrew word as an appositional noun ("Zion, bearer of good news"). Thus, Zion is the bearer of the good news to Judah, not the recipient. She is commanded to climb the high mountain and

---

23. Calvin, *Commentary*, 3:214.

24. Isaiah is the most often quoted biblical book in the work. For a book of reflections on the scriptural texts of Handel's *Messiah*, see Jessica Miller Kelley, *Every Valley: Advent with the Scriptures of Handel's* Messiah (Louisville: Westminster John Knox, 2014).

25. Isaiah 40:6–8 is skipped over in *Messiah*. John F. A. Sawyer, *The Fifth Gospel: Isaiah in the History of Christianity* (Cambridge: Cambridge University Press, 1996), 131, suggests that this omission is because these verses do not appear in the Advent lectionary of the librettist.

lift her voice. The "glad tidings" are not for her. Of course, none of these translational concerns takes away from the beauty of Handel's musical interpretation.

Godspell

The musical *Godspell*, composed by Stephen Schwartz, mostly follows the Gospel of Matthew, so it is no surprise when, after an instrumental prologue, John the Baptist enters the scene and begins to sing "Prepare Ye the Way of the Lord!" He then baptizes the rest of the cast (disciples) as all join in to sing these words repeatedly. What I remember from the Broadway revival of the show I attended in 2012 is the joyful nature of this opening scene. The performance reflected well the tone of the good news as it must have been received by Second Isaiah's audience.

Our Contexts Today

I provide five different contemporary readings of Isaiah 40 now.

Advent

Advent affirms our longing for a better world. The season creates a space to explore how God's transformative work might convert us and our society into more peaceful and just places. Isaiah 40, with its promises of God's deliverance, God's transformation of the landscape, and God's glory revealed, is an Advent song. Under these promises lie a yearning and hope. God's anticipated return from exile and God's continuing presence within the community provide the content for an Advent celebration. What are we longing for this Advent?

Peace Sunday—The Second Sunday of Advent

The Sunday on which Isaiah 40 is read is often celebrated as Peace Sunday; the Peace Candle is lit in the Advent wreath. As we focus on this concept of peace, which is often described in generic terms, how do we present this biblical passage about divine transformation and presence?

I am currently a member of a church that celebrates Peace Sunday with a meaningful and rich ritual. The church has a more-than-twenty-year tradition of placing white wooden crosses on their front lawn—one cross for every life lost to homicide in our city. In the worship services, we read a list of these victims of violence in our city. Since we are in a relatively large metropolitan area, sometimes the list is sadly over a hundred people. At the end of the service, we recess as a church body outside into the chilly winter air and onto the front lawn to hammer white crosses into the frozen ground. It is at that moment that I wonder how Isaiah 40 might be heard alongside the noise of hammers. The comfort of Isaiah 40 is not a quick bandage to create an easy peace. The original audience of Second Isaiah had experienced incredibly debilitating circumstances. Hope and comfort for them were going to require more than rhetoric. Likewise, our contemporary problem of gun violence is not going away quickly. However, we can hope for a world of peace in which God's presence transforms the antecedents to violence. In many ways, I think my church community huddled on the front lawn on Peace Sunday testifies to the feisty hope of Advent. It is just as important, however, that the church take its message of Advent peace and find ways to enact it in our community in tangible ways to reduce the homicide rate before next Advent comes again.

Reading with the Revised Common Lectionary: Mark 1:1–8

The Gospel of Mark begins with a title: "The beginning of the good news of Jesus Christ, the Son of God" (Mark 1:1, New Revised Standard Version). It then immediately contains a quotation from the book of Isaiah (40:3):

> As it is written in the prophet Isaiah, "See, I am sending my messenger ahead of you, who will prepare your way; the voice of one crying out in the wilderness: 'Prepare the way of the Lord, make his paths straight.'" (Mark 1:2–3, New Revised Standard Version)

Many commentators have pointed out that the first half of the quotation (v. 2b) attributed to Isaiah is not Isaiah at all, but Malachi (3:1) and Exodus (23:20). Verse 3, however, does come from Isaiah 40:3 (following the Septuagint translation). Then, Mark introduces John the Baptist, who is "in the wilderness, proclaiming a baptism of repentance for the forgiveness of sins" (Mark 1:4, New Revised Standard Version). Boring provides a coherent reading of how these verses work together:

> In Mark, it is thus all the more clear that God speaks *to* the transcendent Lord (Jesus) *about* the messenger (John), who will prepare *your* (Jesus') way. Before the appearance of either John or Jesus on the historical stage, Mark's hearer-readers know the identity of both, and that John's role is to prepare the way for the Lord Jesus.[26]

John the Baptist in the Mark Gospel reading is a prophet like Isaiah. He is not a fortune teller or foreteller either but a caller for repentance. Both John and Second Isaiah preach about the way of God.

The Gospel

A tendency exists in some contemporary Christian traditions today to speak of the good news or the gospel in spiritual terms alone. Others might relegate the good news to the New Testament and/or Jesus as if the Old Testament cannot be its source. In Isaiah 40 we have the Hebrew word for good news, *basar*. This word is translated in Greek as *euangelion* (literally from a Greek prefix meaning "good" and a word meaning "message"—can you see the word "angel" in it?).[27] This is the Greek word central to the theology of the New Testament. However, the concept is also found in the Hebrew Scriptures, including Isaiah 40. In our passage, the good news is foremost

---

26. Boring, "Isaiah 40:3 to Matthew 3:3," 35.

27. By the way, this word eventually comes through Latin into Middle English as "godspel," which is also a combination of two words meaning literally "good news."

God's presence among the devastated and desolate people. God will come to them as warrior and shepherd; God will deliver them from their oppression. God will deal with the enemy. It is physical liberation. And it is communal. It is not primarily spiritual salvation or individual salvation.

God the Warrior and the Shepherd

Our passage from Isaiah 40 concludes in verses 10–11 by evoking two dissimilar images for God: warrior and shepherd. After Zion announces to the other cities that God is present, the text says that God comes with a mighty arm, invoking an exodus image (Exodus 6:6). God's might will confront the enemies of Judah with power. Then, the passage evokes the image of a shepherd who guards the flock and gathers them. Brueggemann brings the images together thus: "The two verses together, with the twin images of warrior and shepherd and the twin accents of majesty and mercy, bespeak all that is crucial about the good news. [God] is strong enough to emancipate, gentle enough to attend to wants and needs."[28]

A Bifocal Look

With our near vision, we hear Isaiah 40 in the music of Handel. With our near vision, we shout during Advent, "Prepare the way of God!"

With our far vision, we see Isaiah's message of consolation to Jews as they commemorate the destruction of the temple. With our far vision, we think about God's presence to the exiled community of Israel during this anonymous prophet's life.

---

28. Brueggemann, *Isaiah 40–66*, 21.

TEN

Isaiah 64:1–9

First Sunday of Advent in Year B

Open wide your heavens! Let your name be known!
So the world will know, Lord, we are not alone.
You who once did awesome deeds—show your presence here!
Open wide your heavens! Let us know you're near.[1]

¹ Would that you rip open heavens and come down,
mountains would quake at your presence,
² as when fire kindles brushwood
and fire brings water to boil,
to make known your name to your adversaries;
nations will tremble at your presence.
³ When you did wonders we did not hope for,
you came down, mountains quaked at your presence.

⁴ From days of old they have not heard, ear has not perceived,
eye has not seen a God besides you, who works for the one
who waits for God.
⁵ You meet those rejoicing and who do righteousness,
those who remember you in your ways.
Look! You were angry, and we sinned;

we were in them forever, and we will be saved.
⁶ We have become like an unclean thing, all of us,
and all our righteous acts are like a filthy cloth.
We fade like a leaf, all of us,
and our iniquities, like wind, lift us away.
⁷ There is no one who calls on your name,
who rouses to grasp you;
for you have hidden your face from us,
and have handed us over into the hand of our iniquity.

⁸ But, now O Living God, you are our Father;
we are the clay, and you are our potter;
the work of your hand, all of us.
⁹ Do not be very angry, O Living God,
and do not remember iniquity forever.
Behold! Look, we are your people, all of us.²

This chapter first introduces the originating context of Isaiah 64. We then turn to several contemporary contexts, including the Advent theme of hope and a post-Holocaust reading.

The Originating Context of Isaiah 64

Isaiah 64:1–9 is not a distinct literary unit within the book of Isaiah. The passage begins considerably earlier in the previous chapter in 63:7 and continues to 64:12. A switch in the speaker from God in 63:1–6 to a communal voice in 63:7–64:12 and back to God in 65:1 helps to confirm this division. To read only 64:1–9 is to read only the middle section of the overall speech; we do not get the benefit of the introduction or the conclusion. Isaiah 64:1–9 is the lectionary's delineation of this passage; thus, a new artificial literary unit has been created for liturgical purposes. I will comment primarily on 64:1–9

2. The Hebrew and English versifications (division into verses) differ with this passage. Throughout this chapter, I am using the versification of English translations.

with some reference to the entire passage. The overall passage can be divided into two addresses to God by the prophet who speaks for the community: 63:7–14 and 63:15–64:12.

The passage shares many similarities to a psalm of communal lament or complaint.[3] Marvin Sweeney, using Hermann Gunkel's and Sigmund Mowinckel's research, notes the following elements typically contained in a lament: "historical reminiscence, praise of [God], a description of the present unsatisfactory conditions of the people, attempts to motivate [God] to act, a petition, assurance of a hearing, and a commitment to offer a vow or thanksgiving offering."[4] The last two elements in the list are the only two missing in the larger passage, according to Sweeney's analysis. Our focal text, 64:1–9, contains the element of appeal. The prophet petitions God to come down and act. However, the appeal is embedded within a more substantial speech that includes other elements.

Isaiah 64, occurring as a part of Third Isaiah (Isaiah 56–66), is dated to the postexilic period. It does not originate with the prophet Isaiah but the postexilic Judean community, who live under the rule of the Persian Empire. It is a community in need of hope as they attempt to rebuild the temple and leadership after the effects of the Babylonian exile. Third Isaiah struggles with the promises and words of comfort offered in Second Isaiah (Isaiah 40–55) since many of these assurances have not come to fruition yet in the lives of the postexilic community. The passage lacks specific historical references to rulers or events, making it open to later reinterpretations.

Isaiah 63:7–19 contains useful information to inform our reading of 64:1–9. First, the passage begins by telling some of the history of God's saving relationship to the Israelites. God brought them out of slavery in Egypt through the exodus event; God led them through the wilderness even though they rebelled; God brought them into the Promised Land. This type of recitation of past events is typical of the lament genre and forms the basis of the forthcoming appeal. The

---

3. For examples in the Psalms, see Psalm 44, 79, 80, 94. See also the book of Lamentations.

4. Marvin A. Sweeney, *Isaiah 40–66*, The Forms of the Old Testament Literature (Grand Rapids: Eerdmans, 2016), 350.

people remember and recite God's previous actions while sprinkling the speech with questions about God's current presence. For example, 63:11 asks, "Where is the one who brought them up out of the sea?" God has acted in the past so why isn't God acting now? Isaiah 63:15–19 begins the appeal portion of the lament. It takes the form of command at first: "Look down and see." The people question God's presence and why God hardened their hearts. The lament alludes to the destruction of the temple by Israel's adversaries.

Isaiah 64:1–3 continues the appeal directly addressed to God. The imagery of tearing open the heavens, quaking mountains, and kindling fire is one of strength in general but also theophany in particular. The appeal harkens back to God's appearance on Mt. Sinai and recognizes the ancient expectations that accompany the revelation of God to the people. Theophanies occur in Judges 5:4–5 and Psalm 18 as well. The plea to appear here is so that the nations and God's adversaries might tremble and know God's name. It is not an appearance to reveal *torah* as in the Exodus story but to vindicate Israel by punishing her enemies. The tone of this appeal seems critical and pressing.

Isaiah 64:4–7 begins by portraying God as One of action. However, the people have rebelled. They have become unclean and shriveled. The lamenter asks how they can be saved in such a situation of destitution. God has hidden God's face from the people; as a result, the people melt. It is a confession of sin worthy of exploration as the people grapple with their recent experience of exile.

Isaiah 64:8–9 uses the metaphors of father/child as well as potter/clay to speak of the relationship between God and Israel. Earlier in Second Isaiah (45:9–10) the prophetic book also compares God to a potter and father (and mother!).[5] The appeal to "our Father" has occurred previously in this very passage (63:16) and connotes elements of protection and responsibility. It is a rare title for God in the Hebrew Bible but will gain in popularity during Second Temple Judaism.[6] Katheryn Pfisterer Darr reads the potter metaphor as

---

5. Paul will use the potter metaphor in Romans 9:20–21.

6. God is called Father in Deuteronomy 32:6; Psalm 68:5; Jeremiah 3:4, 19; 31:9; Malachi 1:6; and 2:10. For further analysis of this metaphor, see Paul

follows: "Central to these potter/clay metaphors is the potter's . . . absolute control over the clay. Less emphasized, but present nonetheless, is the concomitant notion of the clay's (Israel's) malleability, and hence of the potter's responsibility for the form it assumes."[7] Verse 9 returns to the matter of God's anger and requests that God not remain angry forever at God's people.

The passage continues for three more verses and concludes with a question: "Will you remain silent, and punish us so harshly?" It is an incredible end to this passionate and daring speech but is not included in the lectionary reading. God's response to this lament is contained in Isaiah 65–66 as the conclusion to the book.

Our Contexts Today

I read Isaiah 64 now using eight different contemporary contexts. These contexts address both Christian liturgical and ethical concerns.

Advent

Every First Sunday of Advent—no matter the year—the Revised Common Lectionary includes an eschatological passage for the Gospel reading with complementary readings from the Old Testament and the Epistles. The First Sunday of Advent, therefore, resounds with talk of ends of days. Reading Isaiah 64:1–9 within this context creates the impression that this prophecy too is eschatological in nature. For God to tear open the heavens and come down sounds like an end of the world, and the Gospel reading from Mark 13 helps to confirm this understanding. However, God can manifest without those sorts of connotations. God's revelation does not have to be God's final revelation. In Isaiah 64, the appeal is not for God to come

---

Niskanen, "YHWH as Father, Redeemer, and Potter in Isaiah 63:7–64:11," *The Catholic Biblical Quarterly* (2006): 397–407.

7. Katheryn Pfisterer Darr, *Isaiah's Vision and the Family of God* (Louisville: Westminster John Knox, 1994), 78–79.

down once and for all to end the world in judgment. The petition is for God to appear to right the wrongs, to act again in the lives of a desolate community. We need not allow the Gospel reading to turn Isaiah 64 into eschatology. In fact, it may be more helpful to contrast Isaiah 64 and the Gospel reading as two different ways to think about God's presence.

During Advent, Christians hold in tension both the first coming of Christ and the second coming. It is important to place both of these revelations in the context of the larger biblical story of God's revelation by including prophetic passages that lament the current state of the world and appeal to God to reveal God's self. How shall we call upon God to come down in our communal lives? A song from Cameroon supplies one answer: "He came down that we may have love."[8]

The Hope Candle of Advent

On the First Sunday of Advent, we typically light the Hope Candle. The element of hope is contained in this lament of Isaiah 64 through the appeal to God's past actions of deliverance and presence to God's people. They have hope in a response and a restored sense of divine presence because of God's actions. It is indeed an act of hope to recite God's previous acts of grace and petition again for such actions. As the community gathered during the season of Advent, how should we hope? As we light the Candle of Hope, how might we recall God's actions in our individual and communal lives in order to hope anew that God will act again? Advent calls for a robust hope—an unsettledness with the present reality, as well as an imagined future. It is hope to demand that God come down and save.

The Liturgical Context of the Revised Common Lectionary

The lectionary selects only a portion of this prophetic lament to read. Perhaps the entire passage is too long to read aloud. Difficult deci-

---

8. "He Came Down," (no. 137) in *Glory to God: The Presbyterian Hymnal* (Louisville: Westminster John Knox, 2013).

sions are made when selecting lessons for public reading. However, this particular artificial selection of Isaiah 64:1–9 only demonstrates how this passage is not meant to be read and understood on its own as an independent piece of Scripture. Instead, the passage is edited intentionally by the creators of the lectionary so that it fits with the Gospel reading for this First Sunday of Advent in Year B. Liturgists might preface their reading of this selection with some remarks about the overall literary context. As noted above, Isaiah 64 could also be read in contrast to the more eschatological Gospel readings.

Reading with the Revised Common Lectionary: Psalm 80

The Old Testament, especially the Psalter, contains several communal laments. The contemporary Christian tradition tends to focus more heavily on the psalms of praise and thanksgiving, but an essential theological resource is present in these complaint psalms. The Revised Common Lectionary provides a communal lament in Psalm 80 as the selection for this first week of Advent. This psalm echoes the sentiment of Isaiah 64 by appealing to God, the Shepherd of Israel, to come and save the flock. God is encouraged to make God's face shine so that the people will be saved. Some scholars have posited that this particular psalm was composed in the wake of the 722 BCE destruction of Samaria by the Assyrians. Read together, Isaiah 64 and Psalm 80 then reflect on two of the great historical tragedies of ancient Israel: the destruction of the Northern Kingdom of Israel by Assyria and the destruction of the Southern Kingdom of Judah by Babylon. They lament the loss of kingship, land, temple, and assured understandings of God's activity. So the psalmist pleads at three different points, "Restore us, O God." It is important to remember that Psalm 80 is not lament in anticipation of the end times but actual historical trauma.

Reading with the Revised Common Lectionary: Mark 13:24–37

Mark 13:24–37 occurs within the context of Mark's "Little Apocalypse" (Mark 13:1–37). Mark momentarily turns his attention from telling the events of Jesus's final days in Jerusalem to Jesus's teaching on the last days, that is, the end of the world. The first section of our focal passage speaks of the coming of the Son of Man in clouds. It is an eschatological scene that we are accustomed to hearing on the First Sunday of Advent. The passage concludes with Jesus's statement about not knowing the day when the time will come and an admonition to stay awake.

Isaiah 64 and Mark 13, then, are both concerned with God's presence and manifestation among God's people. In Isaiah, it takes the form of a plea for God to come down, while in Mark it is shaped more by anticipation concerning the final return of a messiah figure. The passages share the historical context of empire as each expects God to judge Israel's enemies. By reading both of these passages within the context of worship during Advent, we can explore how each represents a longing for God's transformative presence.

A Post-Holocaust Reading

Isaiah 64 struggles with God's presence, as Paul Hanson notes: "The remembered past was a time characterized by God's presence in the midst of the people, saving them from the dangers that engulfed them. The present, in contrast, is a time of God's absence, a time of the soul-searching question, 'Where?'"[9] This stunning one-word question still lingers in the wake of the Holocaust. Jewish theology and Jews, of course, wrestle with this question, but Christians must also. God's seeming absence during many of the atrocities of the twentieth century needs a theological and pastoral response. Where were you, God, during our distress?

The Jewish writer and Holocaust survivor Elie Wiesel ventures one response to the question of "Where?" In his classic book *Night*, there is a "Where?" scene. As a child hangs in the gallows of a concentration camp dying, an observer asks, "Where is God? Where is He?"

Wiesel answers, "And I heard a voice within me answer him: 'Where is He? Here He is. . . . He is hanging here on this gallows.'"[10]

---

9. Paul D. Hanson, *Isaiah 40–66*, Interpretation (Louisville: Westminster John Knox, 1995), 237.

10. Elie Wiesel, *Night* (New York: Hill and Wang, 2006), 65. This story is told in Hanson, *Isaiah 40–66*, 237–38.

Wiesel brings together the presence of God and the image of a Jewish child dying in a Nazi concentration camp.

Christians must also answer the question of "Where?" concerning our own tradition's complicity during this period. Where were we when our siblings were being killed by the millions? How do we provide space within our communities to lament such a lack of response? How do we commit to a neighborly love that binds us ethically to our neighbors and their flourishing?

Lament

Contemporary Christian traditions generally do not use lament in worship and spirituality. It remains, however, a valuable resource within the biblical tradition and allows for a response to injustice. Some scholars have suggested that Isaiah 64 was used in temple liturgy.[11] Some form of this chapter may be appropriate as a litany, especially a confession of sin, in corporate worship. It is helpful to think broadly about lament and not see it narrowly as a complaint. To lament is to long. Hanson articulates the theological richness of lament as follows: "The theological assumption that underlies the lament is the steadfastness of God. Within Israel's understanding of the covenant, however, God's mercy was not construed in magical terms but relational ones. God's protection could not be taken for granted but was understood as the blessing granted to a people living in obedience to God's will."[12]

God's Hidden Face

The phrase "hide the face" occurs twenty-nine times in the Hebrew Bible, mostly in the Psalms, and six times in Isaiah.[13] The phrase appears mostly in contexts of judgment for sin and lament. We have seen above that Isaiah 64 takes the form of a lament. Samuel Bal-

---

11. Sweeney, *Isaiah 40–66*, 352.
12. Hanson, *Isaiah 40–66*, 235–36.
13. Samuel Balentine, *The Hidden God: The Hiding of the Face of God in the Old Testament* (Oxford: Oxford University Press, 1983), 45.

entine notes, "Here the emphasis is on the worshipper's complaint that God's action seems unmerited by any sin for which [they] may be guilty. Thus the lament is raised with questions and petitions and protests of innocence."[14] In Isaiah 64 God is accused of hiding God's face from the people before they remind themselves that God is their Father.

A Bifocal Look

With our near vision, we see the robust hope of Isaiah 64 amid Advent.

With our far vision, we reflect with our Jewish neighbors on God's seeming absence and ask, "Where?"

14. Balentine, *Hidden God*, 77.

Bibliography

Achtemeier, Paul J. *1 Peter*. Hermeneia. Minneapolis: Fortress, 1996.

Aelred of Rievaulx. *Homilies on the Prophetic Burdens of Isaiah*. Translated by Lewis White. Cistercian Fathers Series 83. Collegeville, MN: Liturgical Press, 2018.

Alexander, J. Neil. *Celebrating Liturgical Time: Days, Weeks, and Seasons*. New York: Church Publishing, 2014.

———. "A Sacred Time in Tension." *Liturgy* 13, no. 3 (1996): 5–10.

———. *Waiting for the Coming: The Liturgical Meaning of Advent, Christmas, Epiphany*. Washington: Pastoral, 1993.

Allen, Horace T., Jr. "Calendar and Lectionary in Reformed Perspective and History." In *Christian Worship in Reformed Churches Past and Present*, edited by Lukas Vischer. Grand Rapids: Eerdmans, 2003.

Allen, Ronald J., and John C. Holbert. *Holy Root, Holy Branches: Christian Preaching from the Old Testament*. Nashville: Abingdon, 1995.

Balentine, Samuel. *The Hidden God: The Hiding of the Face of God in the Old Testament*. Oxford: Oxford University Press, 1983.

Beaton, Richard. *Isaiah's Christ in Matthew's Gospel*. Cambridge: Cambridge University Press, 2002.

———. "Isaiah in Matthew's Gospel." In *Isaiah in the New Testament*, edited by Steve Moyise and Maarten J. J. Menken, 63–78. London: T&T Clark, 2005.

Ben Zvi, Ehud, ed. *Utopia and Dystopia in Prophetic Literature*. Publications of the Finnish Exegetical Society 92. Helsinki: Finnish Exegetical Society, 2006.

Berkovitz, Elizabeth. "Facing the Truth." *Judaism* 27 (1978): 324–26.

Blenkinsopp, Joseph. *Isaiah 40–55*. Anchor Bible Commentary, vol. 19A. New York: Doubleday, 2002.

Bibliography

Bonhoeffer, Dietrich. *Letters and Papers from Prison.* Enlarged ed. Edited by Eberhard Bethge. New York: Macmillan, 1972.

Borg, Marcus, and John Dominic Crossan. *The First Christmas: What the Gospels Really Teach about Jesus's Birth.* New York: Harper-One, 2007.

Boring, M. Eugene. *1 Peter.* Abingdon New Testament Commentaries. Nashville: Abingdon, 1999.

————. "From Isaiah 40:3 to Matthew 3:3—Intertextuality and Traditionsgeschichte." In *Anatomies of the Gospels and Beyond: Essays in Honor of R. Alan Culpepper,* edited by Mikeal C. Parsons, Elizabeth Struthers Malbon, and Paul N. Anderson, 23–38. Leiden: Brill, 2018.

Boys, Mary C. "The Enduring Covenant." In *Seeing Judaism Anew: Christianity's Sacred Obligation,* edited by Mary C. Boys, 17–25. Lanham, MD: Rowman & Littlefield, 2005.

————. *Has God Only One Blessing? Judaism as a Source of Christian Self-Understanding.* New York: Paulist, 2000.

————, ed. *Seeing Judaism Anew: Christianity's Sacred Obligation.* Lanham, MD: Rowman & Littlefield, 2005.

Brenneman, James E. *Canons in Conflict: Negotiating Texts in True and False Prophecy.* Oxford: Oxford University Press, 1997.

Brown, Raymond E. *A Coming Christ in Advent: Essays on the Gospel Narratives Preparing for the Birth of Jesus: Matthew 1 and Luke 1.* Collegeville, MN: Liturgical Press, 1988.

Brueggemann, Walter. "A Fissure Always Uncontained." In *Strange Fire: Reading the Bible after the Holocaust,* edited by Tod Linafelt, 62–75. New York: New York University Press, 2000.

————. *Isaiah 1–39.* Westminster Bible Companion. Louisville: Westminster John Knox, 1998.

————. *Isaiah 40–66.* Westminster Bible Companion. Louisville: Westminster John Knox, 1998.

————. "Reading from the Day 'In Between.'" In *A Shadow of Glory: Reading the New Testament after the Holocaust,* edited by Tod Linafelt, 105–16. New York: Routledge, 2002.

Calvin, John. *Commentary on the Book of the Prophet Isaiah.* Translated by William Pringle. Grand Rapids: Eerdmans, 1953.

Cartledge, Tony W. *1 & 2 Samuel.* Macon, GA: Smyth & Helwys, 2001.

Bibliography

Childs, Brevard. *Isaiah*. Old Testament Library. Louisville: Westminster John Knox, 2000.

Chilton, Bruce D. *The Isaiah Targum*. The Aramaic Bible, vol. 11. Wilmington, DE: Glazier, 1987.

Clements, Ronald E. "The Messianic Hope in the Old Testament." *Journal for the Study of the Old Testament* 43 (1989): 3–19.

Collins, John J. *The Apocalyptic Imagination*. 2nd edition. Grand Rapids: Eerdmans, 1998.

———. "A Herald of Good Tidings: Isaiah 61:1–3 and Its Actualization in the Dead Sea Scrolls." In *The Quest for Context and Meaning: Studies in Biblical Intertextuality in Honor of James A. Sanders*, edited by Craig A. Evans and Shemaryahu Talmon, 225–40. Leiden: Brill, 1997.

———. *The Scepter and the Star: The Messiahs of the Dead Sea Scrolls and Other Ancient Literature*. Anchor Bible Reference Library. New York: Doubleday, 1995.

———. "The Eschatology of Zechariah." In *Knowing the End from the Beginning: The Prophetic, the Apocalyptic and Their Relationships*, edited by Lester L. Grabbe and Robert D. Haak, 74–84. Journal for the Study of the Pseudepigrapha Supplement Series 46. London: T&T Clark, 2003.

Cone, James H. *A Black Theology of Liberation*. Philadelphia and New York: J. B. Lippincott Company, 1970.

Davis, Ellen F. *Biblical Prophecy: Perspectives for Christian Theology, Discipleship, and Ministry*. Louisville: Westminster John Knox, 2014.

Darr, Katheryn Pfisterer. *Isaiah's Vision and the Family of God*. Louisville: Westminster John Knox, 1994.

Elliott, John. *1 Peter*. Anchor Bible 37B. New York: Doubleday, 2000.

Ericksen, Robert. *Complicity in the Holocaust: Churches and Universities in Nazi Germany*. Cambridge: Cambridge University Press, 2012.

Fisher, Eugene J., and Leon Klenicki, eds. *Pope John Paul II: Spiritual Pilgrimage: Texts on Jews and Judaism*. New York: Crossroad, 1995.

Fishbane, Michael. *The JPS Bible Commentary Haftarot*. Philadelphia: The Jewish Publication Society, 2002.

Frymer-Kensky, Tikva. "A Jewish Look at Isaiah 2:2–4." *Criterion* 41 (Autumn 2002): 20–25.

Garber, Zev, and Bruce Zuckerman. "Why Do We Call the Holocaust

'The Holocaust'?: An Inquiry into the Psychology of Labels." *Modern Judaism* 9, no. 2 (1989): 197–211.

Glory to God: The Presbyterian Hymnal. Louisville: Westminster John Knox, 2013.

Gravett, Sandra, et. al. *An Introduction to the Hebrew Bible: A Thematic Approach.* Louisville: Westminster John Knox, 2008.

Greenberg, Irving. *The Jewish Way: Living the Holidays.* New York: Simon and Schuster, 2011.

Greidanus, Sidney. *Preaching Christ from the Old Testament: A Contemporary Hermeneutical Method.* Grand Rapids: Eerdmans, 1999.

Hanson, Paul D. *Isaiah 40–66.* Interpretation. Louisville: Westminster John Knox, 1995.

Harrington, Daniel. *The Gospel of Matthew.* Sacra Pagina. Collegeville, MN: Liturgical Press, 1991.

Heschel, Susannah. *The Aryan Jesus: Christian Theologians and the Bible in Nazi Germany.* Princeton: Princeton University Press, 2008.

Heskett, Randall. *Messianism within the Scriptural Scrolls of Isaiah.* The Library of Hebrew Bible/Old Testament Studies 456. New York: T&T Clark, 2007.

Hoefler, Richard C. *A Sign in the Straw.* Lima, OH: CSS, 1980.

Hopkins, Denise Dombkowski. "God's Continuing Covenant with the Jews and the Christian Reading of the Bible." *Prism* 3, no. 2 (1988): 6–75.

Isaac, Jules. *The Teaching of Contempt: Christian Roots of Anti-Semitism.* Edited by Claire Huchet-Bishop and translated by Helen Weaver. New York: Holt, Rinehart & Winston, 1964.

Kelley, Jessica Miller. *Every Valley: Advent with the Scriptures of Handel's Messiah.* Louisville: Westminster John Knox, 2014.

Kessler, Edward. *An Introduction to Jewish-Christian Relations.* Cambridge: Cambridge University Press, 2010.

Knitter, Paul F. *Introducing Theologies of Religions.* Maryknoll, NY: Orbis, 2002.

———. *One Earth, Many Religions: Multifaith Dialogue and Global Responsibility.* Maryknoll, NY: Orbis, 1995.

Langmuir, Gavin I. *Toward a Definition of Antisemitism.* Berkeley: University of California Press, 1990.

Lathrop, Gordon W. *Saving Images: The Presence of the Bible in Christian Liturgy*. Minneapolis: Fortress, 2017.

Lindbeck, George. *The Nature of Doctrine: Religion and Theology in a Postliberal Age*. Louisville: Westminster John Knox, 1984.

Levenson, Jon D. *The Love of God: Divine Gift, Human Gratitude, and Mutual Faithfulness in Judaism*. Princeton: Princeton University Press, 2016.

———. *Sinai and Zion: An Entry into the Jewish Bible*. Minneapolis: Winston, 1985.

Lundblad, Barbara K. "O Come, O Come Immanuel (Year A Verses)," Worship Ministries, http://easternsynod.org/ministries/worship/2013/11/27/o-come-o-come-immanuel-yr-a-verses/.

Luz, Ulrich. *Matthew 1–7*. Hermeneia. Minneapolis: Fortress, 2007.

McCarter, P. Kyle. *1 Samuel*. Anchor Bible 8. Garden City: Doubleday, 1980.

McKinion, Steven A., ed. *Isaiah 1–39*. Ancient Christian Commentary on Scripture: Old Testament 10. Downers Grove, IL: InterVarsity, 2004.

Metz, Johannes Baptist. *The Emergent Church*. Translated by Peter Mann. New York: Crossroad, 1981.

Moessner, David P. *Lord of the Banquet: The Literary and Theological Significance of the Lukan Travel Narrative*. Minneapolis: Fortress, 1989.

Moyaert, Marianne. *Fragile Identities: Towards a Theology of Interreligious Hospitality*. Amsterdam: Rodopi, 2011.

Niskanen, Paul. "YHWH as Father, Redeemer, and Potter in Isaiah 63:7–64:11." *The Catholic Biblical Quarterly* (2006): 397–407.

Nolland, John. *The Gospel of Matthew*. The New International Greek Testament Commentary. Grand Rapids: Eerdmans, 2005.

Noth, Martin. *The History of Israel*. 2nd ed. New York: Harper and Row, 1960.

Novenson, Matthew V. *Christ among the Messiahs: Christ Language in Paul and Messiah Language in Ancient Judaism*. Oxford: Oxford University Press, 2015.

———. *The Grammar of Messianism: An Ancient Jewish Political Idiom and Its Users*. Oxford: Oxford University Press, 2016.

O'Day, Gail R. "Back to the Future: The Eschatological Vision of Advent." *Interpretation* 62, no. 4 (October 2008): 357–70.

Pauw, Amy Plantinga. *Church in Ordinary Time: A Wisdom Ecclesiology.* Grand Rapids: Eerdmans, 2017.

Pawlikowski, John. "Accomplishments and Challenges in the Contemporary Jewish-Christian Encounter." In *Removing Anti-Judaism from the Pulpit,* edited by Howard Clark Kee and Irvin J. Borowsky, 29–35. Philadelphia: American Interfaith Institute, 1996.

Peppard, Michael. "Do We Share a Book? The Sunday Lectionary and Jewish-Christian Relations." *Studies in Christian-Jewish Relations* 1 (2005–6): 89–102.

Pietersma, Albert, and Benjamin G. Wright. *A New English Translation of the Septuagint: And the Other Greek Translations Traditionally Included under That Title.* New York: Oxford University Press, 2007.

The Pontifical Biblical Commission. *The Jewish People and Their Sacred Scriptures in the Christian Bible.* Rome: Vatican Press, 2001.

Redditt, Paul L. *Introduction to the Prophets.* Grand Rapids: Eerdmans, 2008.

Rendtorff, Rolf. *Canon and Theology.* Minneapolis: Fortress, 1993.

Roberts, J. J. M. *First Isaiah.* Hermeneia. Minneapolis: Fortress, 2015.

Rubenstein, Richard L., and John K. Roth. *Approaches to Auschwitz: The Holocaust and Its Legacy.* Louisville: Westminster John Knox, 2003.

Rutledge, Fleming. *Advent: The Once and Future Coming of Jesus Christ.* Grand Rapids: Eerdmans, 2018.

Sawyer, John F. A. *The Fifth Gospel: Isaiah in the History of Christianity.* Cambridge: Cambridge University Press, 1996.

———. *Isaiah through the Centuries.* Wiley Blackwell Bible Commentaries. Hoboken, NJ: Wiley Blackwell, 2018.

Scholem, Gershom. *The Messianic Idea in Judaism and Other Essays on Jewish Spirituality.* New York: Schocken, 1971.

Schweitzer, Steven. *Reading Utopia in Chronicles.* The Library of Hebrew Bible/Old Testament Studies 442. New York: T&T Clark, 2007.

Singing the Living Tradition. Boston: Beacon, 1993.

Strawn, Brent A. "And These Three Are One: A Trinitarian Critique of

Bibliography

Christological Approaches to the Old Testament." *Perspectives in Religious Studies* 31, no. 2 (2004): 191–210.

Sweeney, Marvin. *Isaiah 1–39*. The Forms of the Old Testament Literature 18. Grand Rapids: Eerdmans, 1996.

———. *Isaiah 40–66*. The Forms of the Old Testament Literature 19. Grand Rapids: Eerdmans, 2016.

———. *The Twelve Prophets*. Vol. 2. Collegeville, MN: Liturgical Press, 2000.

Theodoret of Cyrus. *Commentaire sur Isaïe III*. Sources chrétiennes 315. Paris: Cerf, 1984.

Troeger, Thomas H. "Lions and Oxen Will Feed in the Hay." In *New Hymns for the Life of the Church: To Make Our Prayer and Music One*, 58. New York: Oxford University Press, 1992.

Tucker, Gene M. "The Book of Isaiah 1–39." In *The New Interpreter's Bible*, edited by Leander E. Keck. Nashville: Abingdon, 2001.

Tull, Patricia K. *Isaiah 1–39*. Macon, GA: Smyth & Helwys, 2010.

Van Ee, Joshua J. "Wolf and Lamb as Hyperbolic Blessing: Reassessing Creational Connections in Isaiah 11:6–8." *Journal of Biblical Literature* 137, no. 2 (2018): 319–37.

West, Traci C. *Disruptive Christian Ethics*. Louisville: Westminster John Knox, 2006.

Wiesel, Elie. *Night*. New York: Hill and Wang, 2006.

Yancey, Philip. *The Bible Jesus Read*. Grand Rapids: Zondervan, 1999.

Zenger, Erich. *Einleitung in das Alte Testament*. Stuttgart: Kohlhammer, 2012.

Zetterholm, Karin. "Jewish Interpretation of the Bible: Ancient and Contemporary." http://bibleinterp.com/articles/2013/zet378014.shtml.

Subject and Name Index

164–67; postexilic context of
Third Isaiah, 165; post-Holocaust
reading, 170–71; Revised Common Lectionary and edited reading, 168–69; Revised Common
Lectionary and Psalm 80 (lament),
169; Revised Common Lectionary's pairing with Mark 13, 169–70

Jacob, 128, 130
Jerome, 6–7, 52, 78, 87
Jerusalem Temple, 95; Isaiah 2 and
the Temple Mount, 127–30, 136;
Isaiah 40 and the commemoration
of *Tisha b'Av*, 156–57
Jewish-Christian relations, 3–5,
39–58; Christian anti-Judaism,
7–8, 40–41, 53–56; and God's
covenant with the Jewish people,
53, 113–14, 120–21, 171; Hanukkah
and Christmas, 91–92; love for
the Jewish neighbor, xii–xiii, 3–5,
39–42; notions of the messiah, 35,
42–47; post-Holocaust, 56–57;
and prophecy-fulfillment paradigm, 21–26, 33–37, 77; relationship between Hebrew Scriptures
and New Testament, 21–26, 49–52;
Roman Catholic teaching on
Jewish readings of the Bible, 46;
supersessionism, 47–53, 120–21
*Jewish People and Their Sacred Scrip-
tures in the Christian Bible, The*
(Pontifical Biblical Commission),
26n, 34n
Jewish Publication Society Tanakh,
118
John Paul II, 121
John the Baptist, 143, 144, 153–55;
and Isaiah 40 imagery, 153–55,
159, 160–61; and John's Gospel,
119; Mark 1 and introduction of,
160–61; and Matthew's Gospel,

105–6, 144, 153–55, 159; the voice
crying out in the wilderness, 119,
153–55, 160–61
John's Gospel, 119
Joshua ben Jehozadak, 112
Joy Candle of Advent, 118–19,
143–44
Judaism, rabbinic: eschatological
interpretations of Isaiah, 117; Isaiah
7:14 interpretation and Hezekiah,
72–73; parable on biblical interpretation, 9; Targum (Aramaic) translation and messianic interpretation
of Isaiah, 100–101
Judaism, Second Temple, 35, 36,
42–47; Isaiah 35 and postexilic
community, 140–42; Isaiah 61
and postexilic Judean community,
111–14; notion of a messiah, 35,
42–47; postexilic context of Third
Isaiah, 165
Justin Martyr, 7, 47, 54, 72–73, 87

King James Version, 64, 88–89, 158

lament: complaint psalms, 169; in
contemporary Christian traditions,
171; Isaiah 64 and communal
lament genre, 165–67, 169, 171–72
Lathrop, Gordon W., 16n, 38
Latin Vulgate, 87, 99
lectio selecta, 32
Leningrad Codex, 11
Lent observance, 17–19, 22
Levenson, Jon D., 55
Lindbeck, George, 16n
"Lions and Oxen Will Feed in the
Hay" (hymn), 105
"Lo, How a Rose E'er Blooming"
(Christmas carol), 33, 34
Luke's Gospel: eschatological and
messianic interpretations of
Isaiah, 115–17, 121–22; Isaiah 9 and

fulfillment of Isaiah, 67, 155; Tree of Jesse in medieval art and cult of, 101–2

Vuchetich, Evgeniy, 133

waiting, as Advent theme, 20–21, 23, 90

"We'll Build a Land" (hymn), 109–10

West, Traci C., 5

Wiesel, Elie, 170–71

World Day of Peace (1972), 136

wreath candles of Advent, 1, 19, 20, 104–5, 118, 143–44, 159–60, 168

Yancey, Philip, 24

Zedekiah, 95

Zenger, Erich, 25–26

Zion, 129, 132, 142, 151, 158, 162

Scripture Index

Scripture Index